Singleness and Marriage after Christendom

AFTER CHRISTENDOM *Series*

Christendom was a historical era, a geographical region, a political arrangement, a sacral culture and an ideology. For many centuries Europeans have lived in a society that was nominally Christian. Church and state have been the pillars of a remarkable civilisation that can be traced back to the decision of the emperor Constantine I early in the fourth century to replace paganism with Christianity as the imperial religion.

Christendom, a brilliant but brutal culture, flourished in the Middle Ages, fragmented in the reformation of the sixteenth century, but persisted despite the onslaught of modernity. While exporting its values and practices to other parts of the world, however, it has been slowly declining during the past three centuries. In the twenty-first century Christendom is unravelling.

What will emerge from the demise of Christendom is not yet clear, but we can now describe much of western culture as "post-Christendom."

Post-Christendom is the culture that emerges as the Christian faith loses coherence within a society that has been definitively shaped by the Christian story and as the institutions that have been developed to express Christian convictions decline in influence.

This definition, proposed and unpacked in *Post-Christendom*, the first book in the "After Christendom" series,[1] has gained widespread acceptance. *Post-Christendom* investigated the Christendom legacy and raised numerous issues that are explored in the rest of the series. The authors of this series, who write from within the Anabaptist tradition, see the current challenges facing the church not as the loss of a golden age but as opportunities to recover a more biblical and more Christian way of being God's people in God's world.

The series addresses a wide range of issues, including theology, social and political engagement, how we read Scripture, youth work, mission, worship, relationships, and the shape and ethos of the church after Christendom.

Thirteen books have previously been published:

Stuart Murray: *Post-Christendom*

Stuart Murray: *Church after Christendom*

Jonathan Bartley: *Faith and Politics after Christendom*

Jo & Nigel Pimlott: *Youth Work after Christendom*

Alan & Eleanor Kreider: *Worship and Mission after Christendom*

---

1 Stuart Murray, *Post-Christendom: Church and Mission in a Strange New World* (Carlisle: Paternoster, 2004), 19.

Lloyd Pietersen: *Reading the Bible after Christendom*

Andrew Francis: *Hospitality and Community after Christendom*

Fran Porter: *Women and Men after Christendom*

Simon Perry: *Atheism after Christendom*

Brian Haymes & Kyle Gingerich Hiebert: *God after Christendom?*

Jeremy Thomson: *Relationships and Emotions after Christendom*

Dan Yarnell & Andy Hardy: *Missional Discipleship after Christendom*

Joshua Searle: *Theology after Christendom*

Andrew Francis and Janet Sutton-Webb: *Sacraments after Christendom*

These books are not intended to be the last word on the subjects they address, but an invitation to discussion and further exploration. Additional material, including extracts from published books and information about future volumes, can be found at https://amnetwork.uk/resources/.

Stuart Murray

Singleness and Marriage after Christendom

Being and Doing Family

Lina Toth

CASCADE *Books* • Eugene, Oregon

Cascade Books
An Imprint of Wipf and Stock Publishers
199 W. 8th Ave., Suite 3
Eugene, OR 97401

www.wipfandstock.com

PAPERBACK ISBN: 978-1-5326-3556-4
HARDCOVER ISBN: 978-1-5326-3558-8
EBOOK ISBN: 978-1-5326-3557-1

Cataloguing-in-Publication data:

Names: Toth, Lina, author.
Title: Singleness and marriage after christendom : being and doing family / Lina
    Toth.
Description: Eugene, OR : Cascade Books, 2021 | Series: After Christendom | In-
    cludes bibliographical references.
Identifiers: ISBN 978-1-5326-3556-4 (paperback) | ISBN 978-1-5326-3558-8 (hard-
    cover) | ISBN 978-1-5326-3557-1 (ebook)
Subjects: LCSH: Home—Religious aspects—Christianity. | Marriage—Religious
    aspects—Christianity. | Singleness—Religious aspects—Christianity. | Families—
    Religious aspects—Christianity. | Sex—Religious aspects—Christianity.
Classification: BT708 .T68 2021 (print) | BT708 .T68 (ebook)

Table of Contents

Introduction

Then his mother and his brothers came to him, but they could not reach him because of the crowd. And he was told, "Your mother and your brothers are standing outside, wanting to see you." But he said to them, "My mother and my brothers are those who hear the word of God and do it." (Luke 8:20–21)

What comes to your mind when you hear such phrases as "marriage and family" or "family values"? Of course, your answer will depend on your background and experience. For people in the West, they are often associated with such words as "Christianity" or "church," or perhaps "traditional" and "conservative." The link between Christianity and family (understood to mean heterosexual marriage and children) has become a defining feature of the church of late Christendom.

The starting point of this book is the turbulent shifts taking place in Western societies and their structures: an exponential rise in single living and alternative family structures, the redefinition of marriage, and the ease and frequency of divorce. Going hand-in-hand with the loss of "traditional" family ways, some perceive these to be a direct threat to the future and the wellbeing of society as we know it. A considerable proportion of Christians also view them as a direct threat to the future and wellbeing of the church.

Yet back when Christianity was very young, its cultural home—the Roman world—was also very concerned with the demise of the traditional family ways which, similarly, were seen as the very basis of the good society. The culprits accused of destroying family and Roman society were none other than the Christians. One of the defining features of their movement was its allegiance to a different kind of a family called the church—something that shocked Jews and gentiles alike. For these early followers of Jesus of Nazareth, such ordering of values was all part of their commitment to a new reality which they referred to as the kingdom of God. Moreover, the radical pronouncements of their leader had challenged the assumption of marriage as the norm and bearing children as an essential aspect of a life well lived. This was a profoundly different understanding of what counted as a good life, and one that clashed with the normative customs of the time.

How did it happen, then, that today's Christianity is so often associated with fixating on marriage and the nuclear family in a way that stands in contrast to the world portrayed in the New Testament? This book seeks to explore this question. I invite the readers to follow the changes in the practice of marriage and singleness, from those early days of the Christian movement to the current cultural climate which by and large still insists that a romantic partner and children are non-negotiable ingredients of a good life—or, in today's parlance, "happiness." I suggest that this vision of what counts as a happy life has been Christianized and developed into a very popular Christian "happiness package." In fact, Christians seem to hold to it stronger than secular society does, pouring a lot of effort into defending and advocating for the centrality of marriage and the nuclear family to the life and future of the church, as well as that of society at large.

Yet such an understanding of happiness, with its focus on the nuclear family, is at odds with both the New Testament's and early Christians' insistence that, for the followers of Jesus, their primary community was to be the new creation called the church. In that light, rather than a cause for alarm, today's surge in the number of single people is actually an opportunity for the church to reconsider both singleness and marriage as distinctly Christian ways of living. However, such reconsideration requires churches to be genuine *communities* which cultivate a more biblical approach to gaining and retaining happiness.

What This Book Is About: Initial Definitions

"What is your book about?" That's a common question for an author working on a project. I had no problems answering it when I was asked in English: my title was clear enough and apparently interesting enough, and I could usually count on a lively conversation to follow. Things were different, however, whenever I was visiting my native country, Lithuania, and was asked this question in Lithuanian. My answer would be much less short and crisp. The problem? The most common word for "singleness" in Lithuanian (and Russian, and in a number of other languages) is the same word that is used for "loneliness." As we shall see shortly, even in languages which do not have a straightforward linguistic link between singleness and loneliness, the assumption of such a connection still lingers. The "colloquial way of thinking seems to rest on the premise that unless you have a romantic partner, you don't have anyone—you are alone and unattached."[1]

So what is, or counts as, *singleness*? For the purposes of this book, the term will refer to the experience of people who consider themselves (and are likely considered by others) to be single. Their singleness may be joyfully chosen, resented, or somewhere in between. They may or may not have children or belong to nuclear families of their own. They may or may not have been married before. They may or may not be dating or in some kind of an intimate relationship. However, in their everyday conversations, and in their own self-identification, they would think of themselves as single persons—or at least more single than coupled.[2] (In church life, there is also the phenomenon of "church singleness," where, although the person is coupled, they are on their own when it comes to any church-related activities.)

Conversely, my usage of the word *marriage* will at times be used interchangeably with "coupledom," and may include any committed, long-term, exclusive, intimate, and presumably sexual relationship between two people, whether that is religiously or legally sanctioned or not. Of course, from a Christian perspective there is something deeply significant about marriage understood as a sacrament, a covenant, or a faithful union of two people before God and God's community—and this will be discussed at appropriate junctures. As we shall see, marriage has changed significantly from the way it was practiced in the Old Testament, to what it meant in the New Testament and early Christian world, to the kind of marriage we think of today. Thinking about marriage theologically is important, especially in today's climate of tensions over such issues as cohabitation, same-sex relationships, or serial monogamy resulting from divorce (although the latter has been largely accepted in many Christian communities by now). However, this book will not delve deeply into the theological significance of the Christian wedding and its lifetime implications. Rather, it will be concerned with actual experiences and perceptions of coupledom, particularly from the perspective of those who want to follow Jesus.

Finally, a word on the definition of *family*—another highly cultural term. Sometimes it helps to consider it in relation to another concept—that of a household, which tends to be understood more functionally, whereas family

1. DePaulo, *Marriage vs. Single Life*, loc. 523.

2. DePaulo, a social scientist, suggests three different ways of defining singleness: legal singleness (one's marital status in the eyes of the law); social singleness (which is how others see the person's relationship status); and personal singleness (the person's own self-description). Although the three may overlap, there are variations, such as with social singleness involving a relationship that is either disregarded by or hidden from others. *Marriage vs. Single Life*, loc. 254–66.

often carries symbolic and ideological overtones.[3] Beyond this general observation, however, family is impossible to describe outside of a specific context. The following chapters will reflect how much the shape and the functions of the family have changed, from extended family and household structures in the world of the Bible to the nuclear family forms of today. And, of course, it is still changing, much to the great anxiety of those who see themselves as defenders of "traditional" family. My focus, however, will be the experience of family in relation to singleness, marriage, and the commitment to what for Jesus clearly was to be the primary community or family of his followers—the church.

What This Book Is Not About

A modest volume such as this one cannot cover everything, especially given the many facets and perspectives that could be employed in exploring singleness, marriage, and family. Inevitably, I had to choose what to focus on, which interpretative lenses to use, and what kinds of questions or aspects of singleness and marriage may need to be left behind.

I have already mentioned that this book is not focused on the theology of marriage as such: there are plenty of other volumes devoted to this topic.[4] The primary interest of this book is the everyday theology which undergirds the way we live as singletons, married couples, or those somewhere in between. I look at these from a broadly Christian perspective, although, not surprisingly for this book series, my particular affinity is with tradition which follows in the footsteps of the Radical Reformation and has the task of the continuous transformation of the intentional community of disciples at its very core. My earlier, academic work on singleness[5] has been focused on this church tradition, although experience and research into other church traditions suggest that they face similar challenges, especially for those single not by a calling, but by life circumstances or a choice based on other than religious grounds.

Much of what I have to say pertains to the cultures which can be increasingly described as "post-Christian." And as post-Christendom is a Western phenomenon, this means that we will have to skip over non-Western contemporary cultures, fascinating as they are. Life in other parts of the world has been, and continues to be, shaped by some other significant factors which

---

3. Moxnes, "What Is Family?," 17.

4. See, for instance, McCarthy, *Sex and Love in the Home*; Instone-Brewer, *Divorce and Remarriage*; Noble et al., *Marriage, Family and Relationships*.

5. Andronovienė, *Transforming the Struggles*.

fall beyond the scope of this work. I do hope, however, that readers from the Majority World may also find this book helpful as they wrestle with the significance of singleness in cultures which typically put the utmost value on extended family and clan allegiance.[6]

Similarly, I will not delve into questions about the role of the church in public issues such as marriage law, important as they may be both for the life of Christian communities and societies as a whole. Other writings explore these questions in detail, although contexts continue to vary greatly.[7] My own perspective, steeped in the Anabaptist tradition, would prefer the severing of the link between church and state when it comes to performing legally binding marriage ceremonies, but readers holding to different positions (or, even more likely, living in different realities) will hopefully see the logic behind this book's focus on two primary ways of organizing personal life which are broadly termed *marriage* and *singleness*—regardless of legal definitions or theological perspectives.

Furthermore, much could be said about gender roles within marriage and the difference that gender makes in the experience of singleness—but again, this is not the focus of the present book. That said, readers will have no trouble recognizing my own stance, which is that of an egalitarian understanding of gender relations on the basis of my reading of the Christian Scriptures. I will occasionally highlight the implications of various historical developments for women—single or married—in particular, as this is an important aspect of the changes which our societies have undergone. For a much fuller picture, however, see another book in the "After Christendom" series: Fran Porter's *Women and Men After Christendom: The Dis-Ordering of Gender Relationships*.

---

6. Indeed, many non-Western societies, whose version of "traditional" family is much closer to the culture of biblical times, face very serious challenges today. In such societies, life can still be organized around a version of a household the central role in which is played by a male elder. Yet change is sweeping through many of these societies too, often due to health, environmental crises, and violence. Different forms of family are emerging, including those headed by women, grandparents, or children, and in some cultures these forms live alongside the ancient tradition of polygamous structures. At the same time, especially in cities, young people are increasingly remaining single. In the African context and its traditional emphasis on ancestor veneration, singleness faces an additional challenge because single people cannot ever become ancestors—in other words, they never become part of their community's enduring story.

7. See, for instance, Nichols, *Marriage and Divorce*; Grzymała-Busse, *Nations under God*. For a brief general overview of the church's relationship to the state, see Murray, *Post-Christendom*.

Who This Book Is For

This particular book is for those who, in one way or another, feel the pull of Jesus and his teaching as portrayed in the Gospels. Some of you may be really frustrated by how much institutional expressions of the church have been shackled to Christendom's constructions and perhaps are able to hold only a tentative relationship with the church. If so, I recognize and share with you the same frustration. Many others interested in this series, or this particular book, are likely continuing their life in a particular Christian community, but also grapple with the tension between the vision of the kingdom of God so powerfully cast by Jesus, and the power of cultural norms, models, and practices which, though present in the church, seem to be at odds with its calling.

Of course, "the church" can mean many things: it can mean a potent institution holding tightly to political influence, or minute gatherings of believers who are marginalized and may be even persecuted by those in power, or—as often is the case in today's Western context—Christian communities of whatever denomination which feel increasingly confused in the rapidly changing world explored in the "After Christendom" series. Indeed, all these different meanings will be touched upon in this volume. At this point, however, it will suffice to say that all church traditions today face similar challenges, and so my hope is that whatever your church belonging (or whatever church you stay away from!), you will find this book helpful.

Other than that, this book is for everyone—younger or older, single, married, in a relationship or somewhere in between. My hope is that single people will be encouraged and heartened to discover how relevant the radical message of Jesus is to living as a single person, and what a gift they are, to the society and to the communities of Jesus. This book is also for married people, not only because it may help them understand how marriage has acquired its current shape, and how it became so strongly wedded to the idea of romantic bliss, but also, I hope, because they will see that singleness needs to be taken seriously if marriage is to be done better. (I may also add that one never knows when and how one's own marital status may change: if anything, singleness is the default position, and one which many of us will experience towards the end of our lives, if not before.)

A Brief Map for the Journey

Here is a brief summary of our journey ahead, which will give you an idea of what to expect from chapter to chapter, and even help you decide where you want to start first.

Chapter 1 outlines the current state of affairs in the early twenty-first century: an exponential rise in the number of single people, the emergence of alternative family structures, and the perceived crisis of the institution of marriage and the "traditional" family model. Next we will look at the ways in which the church reacts to singleness, uncovering the common perception that marriage and the nuclear family are much more important aspects of church makeup and ministry than singleness.

Chapter 2 starts with a sketch of biblical perspectives on singleness, marriage, and family in the world of the Old Testament, which provides the background for how shocking the teaching of Jesus must have seemed on these matters. While the Old Testament assumes marriage as the norm and children as an essential aspect of living well, in Jesus' teaching we observe a radical shift towards the larger context of a new community—that of the followers of the Way of Jesus. His message was radical both in its insistence on the faithfulness-for-life required in marriage, and his even more stunning call for abstaining from marriage as a celebration of God's Kingdom. It is his hard-to-swallow teaching that we will take as the starting point for our understanding of singleness and marriage today, however much our twenty-first-century realities differ from the ancient world of first-century Palestine.

In order to help with this task, chapter 3 broadens the picture to how families and households functioned in the Greco-Roman world in which the first Christians found themselves, and in which the New Testament writings were born. We will look at the tensions over Roman "family values," the legislation that required Roman citizens to marry, and the disruption which Christians brought into the mix. We will survey the major New Testament passages on singleness, marriage, and household life, and see how the first churches both confronted and adapted to the societal norms of the time.

Looking at the earliest Christian literature outside of the New Testament, chapter 4 surveys the frequent hostility with which the authorities, and indeed society as a whole, treated the Christian movement for its perceived destabilization of society and its established order. The starkest example here was the spread of Christian asceticism and celibacy—a reflection of how strongly those believers yearned for the fullness of times and the arrival of God's kingdom. As we trace the story of those early Christian centuries, we will see conflicting visions for what counted as the best life possible, but also an increasing "hierarchy of holiness" which placed virginity at the top and considered marriage as its inferior.

Chapter 5 explores how marriage and single life continued to change once Christianity emerged as the official religion of the empire. We will trace the surge of monasticism, its subsequent development, and the eventual enforcement of celibacy for the priests. However, we will also look at other, less-known forms of singleness of medieval Europe, such as the story of lay women's communities called the Beguines. We will then turn our attention to the development of the theology and practice of marriage and its gradual Christianization.

Chapter 6 takes us first through the changes brought on by the Reformation movements, including the Anabaptists and their desire to recapture the New Testament teaching of the church as primary family. Moving on to the impact of the Industrial Revolution, we will look at some attempts to rethink singleness, marriage, and family life, and particularly the emergence of the Victorian family model. While the twentieth century saw the Victorian family ideal shaken and battered by wars, radical social movements, the massive employment of women, effective contraception, and the sexual revolution, its appeal as a representation of a God-given order for Christians still lingers.

Chapter 7 considers the perception of romantic love and the nuclear family as essential components of a "happy" life, and explores how this idea shapes church attitudes towards marriage and singlehood. We will see that the allure of romance has undergone a significant transformation, from its medieval image of an unattainable or tragic love story, to an expectation of undying romance in marriage. We will then investigate the growing preoccupation of our societies with happiness and its related concepts, such as human flourishing, wellbeing, and a meaningful life, and the (prevalent, but contested) assumption that coupledom is the most important source of happiness and fulfillment.

Finally, chapter 8 draws together some key ideas for a "happy" Christian life in the increasingly post-Christian context. If we are to get any closer to the vision of Jesus for singleness and marriage for those who seek the kingdom of God, we face the challenge of churches (or other intentional Christian groupings) having to be real, rather than merely proclaimed, *communities*. As this is no small task in our fragmented, consumeristic culture, we will consider some changes that can be made in order to align our perceptions about singleness and marriage with what we find in the teaching of Jesus. We will consider the importance of the practice of friendship as well as some ways to address our feelings and attitudes towards sexual fulfillment. We will conclude with considering the complex nature of human happiness from a Christian perspective: the importance of creativity, the presence of adversity or suffering, and the work of meaning-making in various life circumstances.

Readers who want a quick sense of the argument will probably want to look at the first two and the last two chapters, and perhaps save the historical review of the development of singleness and marriage throughout the

Christian centuries for a later time. Others will find a more chronological journey from the origins of our faith to the current frameworks more helpful. I have tried to do my best in minimizing technical jargon, but have provided some pointers to further readings on some of the major ideas and issues in the footnotes.

1

Uncharted Territory

Single Households and the Crisis of the "Traditional" Family Model

The State of Affairs: Statistics and Categories

Although there is evidence in a multitude of national contexts showing that singles are being discriminated against less and less, individuals are still socialized and educated to get married and strive to build stable family type units. As a result, singlehood has largely been and still frequently viewed negatively in the eyes of both society and the individual, and in some cases particularly for women.[1]

A few years ago I wandered into a china shop, and there I came across a collection of six different glasses for six kinds of drinks. The box had a picture of a Buddha-like woman with six hands. In each of her hand she was holding a glass for a different drink.

Maybe I should have bought that box, because it represented the very change I am exploring in this book. It would be difficult to imagine such a consumer item selling half a century, or even just a few decades, ago: something designed for the pleasure of one person and their one-person household. Now, however, the market for goods aimed at single people is booming: single-portion ready-meals in supermarkets; L-shaped snuggle pillows; smaller living spaces, solo travel packages, and so on. Technology has been an important

1. Kislev, "Happiness," 2246.

factor in enabling such changes, but so have society's attitudes, and business has been catching up with the demand.

Statistics tells us of a striking, and continuing, increase of single people and single-person households throughout the Western world. In many countries, such as the United States or United Kingdom, single people now comprise about half of the population—a 50 percent rise since mid-twentieth century.[2] In the United States, people now spend a greater proportion of their adult lives single than married.[3] The trend is expected to continue: it is estimated that, compared to 2018, the proportion of single people in Europe, for instance, is going to rise by another 30 percent by 2030.[4] People are also marrying later, and, although the divorce rate has somewhat recovered from its all-time high a few decades ago, it has been partly due to people cohabiting, rather than marrying, in the first place.[5]

The mention of cohabitation, however, is a reminder that statistics does not paint the whole picture. Cohabiting is on the rise, representing almost 20 percent of the population in the United Kingdom and Australia and just over 20 percent in Canada.[6] Yet the fastest-growing household type in many Western countries is that of a single-person household. In the United States, the proportion of solo households has doubled over the last fifty years, and in Nordic countries such as Sweden and Norway around half of all people now live on their own.[7] Of course, a small proportion of couples may be running two households (sometimes referred to as "living apart together"), but a much greater proportion of single people are likely to live with parents, share a household with housemates or friends, or raise children as single parents.

All of this is to say that although the distinction between "married" and "single," or "coupled" and "solo" is not always clear-cut, the general trend is undeniable: marriage rates are falling, and while cohabitation is on the rise, single living is also soaring. More and more people are embracing their single status, with the media increasingly zooming on "single-positive" and "self-partnered" celebrities and trends.[8] Importantly, such attention also points to the changing attitudes towards the ingredients required for happiness and fulfillment—an important theme later on in this book.

2. United Nations, "World Marriage Data 2019."

3. DePaulo, *Marriage vs. Single Life*, loc. 278.

4. Quintos, "Loner Living."

5. Hawkins and Vandenberghe, "Divorce Rates Are Falling."

6. "The Legality of Cohabitation."

7. Ortiz-Ospina, "Rise of Living Alone."

8. Cernik, "Self-partnered."

Another area of great change is the diversification of family types. Beside two-parent and single-parent families, other units are described by such terms as "blended," "binuclear," or "step-families." Same-sex couples are now able to legalize their relationship in a number of countries, and may be raising children together. Adult children are often staying at home for much longer than in the past decades. Where economic emigration is rife, a parent may be working abroad, and the children may be mainly reared by a grandparent. We may also note alternative arrangements, such as polygamy amongst some Utah Mormons, recently given a boost by the amendment to Utah's law against bigamy.[9] Polyamorous relationships—that is, romantic or sexual bonds between more than two people—are more openly practiced and discussed in culture at large, and are beginning to gain attention in the context of the church too.[10] Such changes reflect a growing degree of cultural acceptance of different family models.

All of this may feel completely unprecedented, and disorientating—and in a number of aspects, it is indeed. On the other hand, the chapters that follow will point out that for much of the history of the West, societies have often worried about the "demise" of marriage and family values, that there have been different family models practiced in the past, and that a significant number of people never married, or spent much of their life unmarried.[11] If anything, it is the years following the World War II until the 1970s that are unusual in their assumption of marriage and nuclear family model as the norm for more or less everybody. This is the main reason why the current growth of single population feels unprecedented.

The departure from the nuclear model—often termed the "traditional family"—has given cause for great concern and the urge to fight for what is sometimes called "family values." We will explore the development of the "traditional family" in the subsequent chapters, but what is striking to note at this point is the deep connection that is assumed to exist between Christianity, marriage, and the "traditional family." Indeed, for some people they represent "the historic pillars of Western civilization," currently "under siege and crumbling."[12] Moreover, they are assumed to be central not only to Christian faith, but also to be "fundamental blocks of human society" as a whole.[13] Thus everything else that may be wrong with modern life—social ills or unrest,

9. Grossman and Friedman, "Two's Company."

10. Sprinkle and Parler, "Polyamory."

11. De Groot et al., *Single Life and the City.* For the British account, see Thane, *Happy Families*, 9.

12. Winnail, "Marriage and Family," para. 3.

13. Winnail, "Marriage and Family," para. 3.

poverty, and so on—can be pinned to the purported demise of the "traditional family" and its values.

Marriage as a Norm, Singleness as an "Issue"

> If you are older than thirty-five and not coupled, it is easy in this cultural milieu to internalize the belief that you can't love, are neurotic, and have *issues*.[14]

And yet, although marriage and family values are often perceived to be under attack, in reality they continue to enjoy a strikingly privileged position in the society. Nowhere is it clearer than in comparison and contrast to singleness. In a number of languages, singleness is used to describe the state of being "unmarried"—which, given that the single state comes before a possible married state, is rather curious: "why aren't married people called unsingle?"[15] Singlehood is still commonly seen as something abnormal or unusual, except as a short temporary stage before marriage, or between marriages, or after the death of a spouse. People may be increasingly opting to stay single, but "the notion of singleness as a deviant category seems remarkably enduring."[16]

It is not only those who are married who are projecting such attitude. A significant proportion of single people themselves would prefer to be married, and therefore see their own singleness as something undesired. I have written about different attitudes to one's own singleness (particularly that of women) elsewhere,[17] but here would simply note that it falls somewhere in between treating it as an absolute tragedy on the one end, and joyous embracing of single living as one's preferred choice on the other. There are many nuances on this continuum, and one's reactions or attitudes are not necessarily fixed: one can be *mostly* happy as a single person, but at times feel a tinge of loneliness or sadness of missing out on some aspects of life. (One can also be mostly happily married, but at times long for some aspects of singlehood—except that, as we will see, certain ideological hues make this a much more daring observation or confession.)

With some simplification, however, it is important to recognize both ends of the spectrum. I start with those who would really wish to be married, but have so far struggled to find a suitable partner. When the desire for a

---

14. Trimberger, *New Single Woman*, xi. Emphasis in the original.

15. DePaulo and Morris, "Singles in Society and in Science," 58.

16. Reynolds, *Single Woman*, 152.

17. Andronovienė, *Transforming the Struggles*, 26–36.

partner is combined with a desire for having children of one's own, gender plays an important role, making it a much more poignant question for women. The ticking clock of fertility can make the experience of singleness much more distressing for those who long to have children and raise them together with their father. Technology is presenting some new opportunities (as well as ethical quandaries), and more and more women are opting for artificial insemination, IVF, or are "choosing to freeze their eggs . . . because they have not met the person they would like to have children with."[18]

While reproductive matters can indeed make involuntary singleness a painful experience, in the later chapters I will suggest that a great deal of the anguish about being single arises out of the powerful cultural message most of us have been socialized into. Everyone is supposed to dream of falling in love, marrying, having children, and living happily ever after. No matter how many singles there may be around, one's own singleness may still feel like a rude abnormality. Again, this message of romance and marriage as the norm has a particular hold on women: "the dominant cultural storyline for the lives of women is one of marriage and family relationships."[19] Such perceptions are particularly strongly felt in more conservative settings, such as in the southern United States: "It doesn't matter how successful you [as a woman] are in your career—or how unsuccessful your man is. If you're not married you're a loser."[20] But the necessity of being married comes to catch up with men too, only perhaps a little later: past forty, the bachelor starts losing his appeal unless he "settles down" and becomes partnered.

What is also interesting is that those who embrace their singleness and choose it freely are likely to be viewed more negatively than those who profess their unhappiness about being single, and their desire to marry.[21] It is okay to have "failed" (so far), as long as one continues to affirm the standard of coupledom. For the same reason, widows tend to be viewed more positively and sympathetically than always-single women, because their singleness is perceived to be beyond their control "and because they had 'succeeded' in marriage before the death of their spouse."[22]

As marriage displays such strong ideological overtones, some social scientists have been keen to point out the prevalence of "singlism"—social and economic discrimination and stigmatizing of singles.[23] Discrimination

18. Bearne, "Single Women Are Spending Thousands," 48.
19. Reynolds, *Single Woman*, 74.
20. Fields, "*Atlantic* Got It Wrong.," para. 3.
21. Kislev, "Happiness," 2246.
22. Wadsworth, "Marriage and Subjective Well-Being," 1046.
23. DePaulo, *Singlism*; Byrne and Carr, "Caught in the Cultural Lag," 84–91.

has also been found, for instance, in medical decision-making, with medical professionals assuming that divorced people had less social support than their married counterparts, and therefore less likely to, say, be good transplant patients.[24]

As financial incentives and other privileges for married couples are so common that they are indeed difficult to notice, here is a vivid reverse example from Bella DePaulo, a social scientist and singleness advocate:

> How long would married people put up with their experiences, and how long would it take social scientists to include them as members of a stigmatized group, if their lives included the following:
>
> - Every time you get married, you have to give expensive presents to single people.
>
> - When you travel with your spouse, you have to pay more than when you travel alone.
>
> - When you tell people you are married, they tilt their heads and say things like, "aaaawwww" or "don't worry honey, your turn to divorce will come."
>
> - You get paid less than single people for the same work.
>
> - Single people can add another adult to their health care plan; you can't. . . .
>
> - When you browse the bookstores, you see shelves bursting with titles such as "If I'm So Wonderful, Why Am I Still Married," and "How to Ditch Your Husband After Age 35 Using What I Learned at Harvard Business School."
>
> - Moreover, no one thinks there is anything wrong with any of this.[25]

As reflected in the beginning of this chapter, slowly—very slowly—attitudes in society are starting to shift. Increasing awareness, advocacy, and business opportunities amid the sheer numeric growth are beginning to make a difference, especially among the younger generations. But what about Christian communities?

---

24. Marotta and Ladin, "Marital Privilege."
25. DePaulo and Morris, "Singles and the Scholars Who Study Them."

Singleness in the Church: A Brief Look at the Numbers

> The churches seem to cater much better for
> married than single people, particularly single men.[26]

Let us start with some general observations about singleness in today's church-es. Hard figures are difficult to obtain and vary greatly. For instance, churches in urban settings, especially in university towns, will usually have much high-er proportion of single adults than the congregations in the suburbs or rural areas. A lot depends on how the particular church or denomination views cohabitation, same-sex relationships, and so on, as well as on who is counted as a "Christian" or "church goer" in the studies. Overall, however, there are significantly fewer singles in the church than in society in general. Less than 25 percent of active churchgoers in the United States are single—twice less than in the population at large.[27] A study from the United Kingdom suggests that only around 30 percent of practicing Christians are unpartnered.[28] What-ever variations among different denominations and contexts, it confirms the reality many singles witness on the ground: the church envisions itself as a place for (nuclear) families, with single people representing a smaller, though still sizeable demographic group which often appears invisible to others.

There is another important factor to take into account for the church context: more often than not, there will be a lot fewer men than women. Two women to one man is quite a common ratio, especially among the singles.[29] Some denominations may not have such a pronounced gender imbalance, and some specific congregations have a shortage of women rather than men, but overall, the prevalence of women in churches is starkly consistent across dif-ferent contexts, and does not seem to be dependent on whether the congrega-tion is doctrinally conservative, or ordains women, etc.[30] "The evidence . . . is cumulative: in enquiry after enquiry, the predominance of women is not only affirmed, but striking."[31] Men's participation in church activities on the whole is also more likely to be at a lesser level compared to that of women (ministers and preachers excluded). And with the increase of age, the ratio of single women to single men tends to grow exponentially.

26. Professor Linda Woodhead (Lancaster University, UK), in "Research Co-funded," para. 6.

27. Chiu, "Single-Minded Church," para. 1.

28. "Research Co-funded," fig. 1.

29. Pullinger, "Where Are All the Men"; Stone, "Sex Ratios."

30. Stone, "Sex Ratios."

31. Berger et al., *Religious America, Secular Europe*, 110.

In other words, the majority of single people in the church are female. For heterosexual women who take their Christian faith seriously, that entails a serious possibility of ending up without a partner, or at least without one who would share their faith. For some of them, it becomes the final straw leading to leaving the church altogether.[32]

Why is this so, and can anything be done about it? This is certainly an important question to ask. What would help more men to connect with the church? Can we look deeper at the language we use to talk about relating to God, for example? Or could we explore how and why the current shape of church life and its activities is geared more toward women? However, the greater prevalence of women in church is nothing new, and is not likely to disappear any time soon.[33] It is, in other words, a different problem than the one which is the focus of this book, although there are overlapping issues connecting the two.

Although more men in the churches would be a really welcome development, not the least for the single Christian women desiring to find a male partner who would share their faith, it is not going to "solve" the "issue" of singleness. Rather, a careful look at the church's typical reaction to single people indicates there is a problem: a problem that is not with singleness, but with the actual theology of the church which overwhelmingly favors marriage over singleness.

Singleness in the Church: Singles' Perspectives

> Singleness in the church is a double cross for many Christians to bear as they are both isolated within the church and without because of the different relational values that are practised in normal society.[34]

So what do single people say about the reception they find in churches? Overall, things do not look good. Yes, some singles do find welcoming communities: "My church is (unusually) affirming of ALL its members from the tiniest to the oldest, whether single or married. Whole body ministry is encouraged."[35] While such communities can be acknowledged and celebrated, my focus here is on a disturbingly widespread experience of exclusion. Common words and

---

32. Gaddini, "Why Are So Many Single Women Leaving the Church?"

33. Berger et al., *Religious America, Secular Europe?*, 109–22.

34. "Do Single Christians Feel Part of Their Churches?," para. 125.

35. "Do Single Christians Feel Part of Their Churches?," para. 13.

phrases that many singles use are "being ignored," "viewed with condescension," "treated as if not complete as a person," and, in the case of single women especially, "treated as threats to couples."[36] Those who are single by choice can be simultaneously pitied because they are "lonely," and viewed as selfish (because not wanting to be married is somehow a sign of egotism).

Gina Dalfonzo, a North American writer reflecting on her own context, suggests that the reactions towards singles in the church tend to fall into four categories: singles as problems; singles as pariahs; singles as projects; and then, finally and hopefully, singles as people to be cherished for who they are.[37] "A lot of time," she writes, "the church simply doesn't know what to do with the single and childless."[38] Whether relegated to a singles' group or ignored, they represent an "issue," and a deviation from the norm.

Survey after survey reveals that the church is primarily perceived as a place for marriages and families. We will turn to the official teaching in a moment, but the endorsement of marriage as a norm first of all seeps through the patterns of socializing and communal moments of recognition. "Coupling"— that is, relating as couples—is often the standard pattern, and can be especially difficult to come to terms with for those who had been part of the group, but after becoming single find themselves outsiders. Here is a comment of one widow: "Not only was I excluded from their [coupled] gatherings, but the wives were cautious about developing friendships [with me] . . . It was a bitter pill to swallow when I realized that I was on the other side now and simply did not 'belong' anymore."[39]

Various rites of passage are enthusiastically celebrated, such as marriages, marriage anniversaries, and the blessing of the infants—"but there's really nothing that we do to celebrate any of the events in a single person's life."[40] The implicit (and at times explicit) message is clear: there is nothing to celebrate unless one becomes married. Instead, a single person can expect to be offered (or be subjected to) matchmaking, inquiries as to why she or he is still single, and wishes for "happiness" (read: love and marriage). Many single Christians have their collection of such stories which range from mildly humorous to absolutely awful.

As traditional Christian ethics restricts sexual activity to marriage, singles can experience an enormous pressure to marry so that they do not compromise their sexual purity—a theme we will return to in chapter 8. Until, or

---

36. Brown, "Isolated."

37. Dalfonzo, *One by One*, 27–80.

38. Dalfonzo, *One by One*, 12.

39. Sheridan, *Unwilling Celibates*, 16.

40. Response of an interviewee, in Goering and Krause, "Odd Wo/Man Out," 217.

unless, they marry, the whole teaching on single believers' sexuality can often be summarized in one word: "Don't." But the moment one enters marital bliss, things are expected to fall in place, the bodily desire to switch on and be ready to enjoy the pleasures of marital bed. The results can be tragic: "Purity culture taught me shame. It taught me to be ashamed of my body and ashamed of my desires. I carried that shame into my marriage."[41]

Even for a perfectly content single person, this is a pressurized atmosphere to endure. And as for those perplexed about why God is not answering their prayers for a partner in life, there is even more anguish: "What is wrong with me?" "Why is God not alleviating my suffering?" "Does God love me and bless me less than my friends who are getting married?" "Does it mean that I do have the gift of singleness—but if so, why can't I feel it?" "Have I done something wrong—is God punishing me?" Unsurprisingly, many churches struggle to offer coherent or helpful responses to such questions. What then is typically taught and preached on marriage and singleness?

For the Bible Tells Me So: Teaching and Preaching on Singleness and Marriage

I found going to church one of the loneliest places in the world. That is why I no longer attend. I worship my Lord and Saviour outside the established church.[42]

We will take an in-depth look at the New Testament theology of singleness and marriage in the next chapter, but at this point let us take a brief look at how Scripture is used in discussing marriage and singleness, and what kind of theology is communicated in contemporary churches. I ask the reader to bear in mind that the following observations are, inevitably, generalizations, and do not reflect the variety likely to be found within Christ's body. A more detailed study is available in my earlier work,[43] but here I present some of the most common approaches which highlight the extent of the problem with attitudes towards singleness.

Although the New Testament discusses singleness explicitly, those passages tend to fall into the category of carefully ignored texts. Take, for example, a text as unambiguous as Paul's appeal to the superiority of single life in 1 Corinthians 7:8–9: "To the unmarried and the widows I say that it is well for

41. Sorrell, "Dangers of Purity Culture," para. 9.

42. Single respondent, in "Do Single Christians Feel Part of Their Churches?," para. 42.

43. Andronovienė, *Transforming the Struggles*, 43–50.

them to remain unmarried as I am. But if they are not practicing self-control, they should marry. For it is better to marry than to be aflame with passion." Unsurprisingly, this does not tend to be the choice text for marriage services! It is a rare appearance in the preachers' repertoire at any time of church life, and when it is used, listeners will not likely be urged to stay single in order to be spared "distress in this life" (1 Cor 7:28). Yet Paul's next remark—"if you marry, you do not sin" (1 Cor 7:28)—might get a mention.

Aspects of love, family or marriage, on the other hand, are among the most popular sermon themes and special talk series, whether to celebrate the mystery of the union that is marriage, or to express concern over the culture of divorce and family breakdowns. The assumption is typically made that preaching or teaching on these topics is applicable to all. If a preacher happens to remember that not everybody is married, then perhaps a few words on singleness as a temporary stage will be tagged on. Here is an example: "We had a series on Song of Songs, which covered the subjects of marriage and sex, but without much reference to singleness (except in the form: 'If you're not married, this is how it will be when you are . . .')."[44]

What is at times introduced positively is the notion of the "gift" of single-ness (although it prompts some to pray fervently that they be spared that par-ticular gift). Indeed, taking the gift of singleness seriously should underscore that singles are not second-rate people, but rather persons with a different kind of a calling.[45] But how is this gift to be used? Surely it is about serving God's purposes and God's church, yet the range of such a service can be very narrow. A missionary? No problem; we might even consider supporting her. A senior pastor or leader in the church? Much less likely. Here we stumble upon a rarely verbalized assumption that singleness somehow signals the lack of ba-sic qualification certifying one's maturity and suitability to lead and shepherd others. Such an attitude is especially characteristic of the churches which have been born during or after the Reformation, as they have generally rejected the idea of the calling to the religious life as an alternative to marriage. There may be important lessons to learn from those who practice consecrated celibacy, such as the Catholic and the Orthodox. Indeed, "it is a sad fact that today, many evangelical churches would not permit John the Baptist, Paul or Jesus Himself even to lead a house group, because they are not married (they would probably ban Peter too, as he spends too little time with his family!)."[46]

At the same time, it is important to bear in mind that consecrated celibacy, or "the gift of singleness," is different from what could be termed

44. Aune, *Single Women*, 48.

45. Harding, *Better Than or Equal To?*, 34.

46. Chilcraft, *One of Us*, 121.

involuntary singleness, or singleness by circumstance. In fact, one of the most confusing claims is assuming that unless one has been granted the gift of singleness by God, then surely God has plans for that person to marry. The result is the platitudes such as, "God has planned someone special for you; just wait patiently." Or—perhaps even worse—"Is there something wrong (with you)? Is there an unconfessed sin in your life which is a barrier to God sending you a spouse?"

I could go on. But hopefully the above has already provided more than enough for us to acknowledge that there is a problem, and one that does not have an easy press-one-button solution. While there are wonderful exceptions of acceptance and welcome, too often we seem to be wrestling with a deeply ingrained belief that marriage brings happiness in the way that singleness cannot—a belief present even in the most well-intended teachings on singleness.

Making Sense of What We Truly Believe:
Beyond Declarations

> It is better; it's Paul isn't it, that says it's better to be single um so um, so I think it probably is. But then having said that I think it's really good it's just fun—it's great to be married um, and I think it's a natural thing and I think, you know, you'd expect for most people to get married in the end.[47]

Some of the church attitudes could, perhaps, be attributed to the lack of awareness and reflection. One of the things that struck me when first researching singleness was the churches' obliviousness to how many of their members were single, let alone that their singles typically represented an even greater proportion of society. In my public talks, or conversations with acquaintances and friends about the basic statistics of their church, I commonly encountered their surprise once they have counted and realized what a significant proportion of their community are single: "I had not realized this! We need to do something about it!"

With singleness becoming more prominent in society, more churches are beginning to look more attentively at their own membership or attendance make-up: and that is a good start. Yet "doing something about it" is quite a challenge, even for those who agree that the situation needs to be addressed. Helpful research and recommendations for the greater inclusion of singles

---

47. A Pentecostal pastor, quoted in Aune, "Singleness and Secularization," 63.

into the fabric of faith communities have been available for more than thirty years, but very little change has been seen on the ground.[48]

The reason for this, I contend, is that in the apparent slowness of the church to wake up to the presence of single people in its midst there is something deeper yet than the lack of knowledge or understanding. It is to do with our deep-seated beliefs about the importance of the link between church and marriage. In the climate of marital breakdowns and changing family patterns, a lot of effort is put into emphasizing the importance of the institution of marriage and family as a necessary element of keeping the church going and growing. It is not difficult to see how easily such efforts lead to a disregard of the growing numbers of singles, and a perception of singleness as a threat to the institution of marriage and, by extension, the church itself.

Furthermore, Christian singleness presents a challenge to a very specific notion of happiness which has been embraced and "baptized" without quibbles. In the words of another author, commenting on her own, North American, context: "The church has bought into [the] claim that the well-lived life is the one that has romance and sex at its center; we've just given it a spiritual sanction called marriage."[49] As our society is still fixed on coupledom, most Christians assume that marriage is an essential part of the package of a happy and fulfilled life. Chapters 6 and 7 will look in more detail at how we have adopted such a worldview.

Yet deep down many of us know that coupled happiness is not guaranteed to last: there are too many stories of loss and grief taking place to be oblivious to the fact. But while we know it, we may not like to be reminded of it—and that helps explain why singles experience shunning and exclusion, particularly in social interaction with married Christians: "singleness of others is a reminder that the same dreaded fate may come [one's own] way."[50] Of course, rarely, if ever, is it expressed in such a crude way—and herein lies one of the greatest problems. What we *say* we think, or what we *think* we believe, is not necessarily what we actually *live* by.

Take, for instance, the link between the way we read Scripture and the views we already hold on such matters as happiness, sexuality, or marriage. It is not that Christians particularly object to what Jesus had to say about forgoing marriage for the sake of the kingdom of God. But it turns out that even those who claim to follow everything the Bible says (or Jesus commands, or Paul teaches) may live by a rather different theology which easily disregards the key points of the message. The following two chapters will highlight how

48. See, e.g., Chilcraft et al., *Single Issues*, 39; and "Single-minded."

49. Hitchcock, *Significance of Singleness*, xxi.

50. Patterson, "Singles and the Church," 49.

highly singleness was valued in the New Testament and in life of early church, so the contrast between the New Testament stance and the actual attitudes toward singleness and marriage in today's church will be even starker. At this point, we may simply note the disconnect between the ideas that are consented to intellectually, and the ones that are lived out practically.

Interest in what takes place outside people's declared beliefs has been gaining a lot of traction recently. Thus, in sociology of religion, researchers talk of "lived religion."[51] Practical theologians often employ a term "ordinary," "pastoral," or "lived" theology.[52] Some other theologians point to the fact that most of the time, we are actually unaware of the convictions which drive our own lives. Moreover, different, and even conflicting, convictions can coexist within persons and communities because they are fostered by different groups influencing the person (or a community).[53]

If we really want to understand why Christians react or behave in a particular way, we will need to look beyond the explicit and intentional teaching by way of sermons, Bible studies, or seminars. A large portion of the iceberg of individual or communal convictions will lie under the water, unarticulated and often unknown to the very people who carry them. The clues will be in the testimonies, songs, conversations, and gossipy comments on the lives of others; in the practices people engage in (or avoid); and in the expressions of people's loyalties: what are they willing to expend their energy, time, and money for? Exploring these questions will help us understand the actual convictions we and others carry: not what we *claim* we believe, or even what we *want* to believe, but what we *actually* feel, fear, long for, and believe, deep down, in our gut, so to speak.

Yet what is felt or believed deep down is not necessarily true: Scripture tells us as much. As we travel through the next few chapters, we will explore how much the "Christian happiness package" and its association of church, marriage, and nuclear family clashes with the vision of Jesus and the mission of his community. A profound change of convictions is in order if we are to be faithful to this vision in the world after Christendom. In Christian language, such change is sometimes called conversion. Although it is often associated with a change of heart and mind in the beginning of someone's faith journey,

51. See, for example, McGuire, *Lived Religion*.

52. See, for instance, Astley and Francis, *Exploring Ordinary Theology*; Marsh et al., *Lived Theology*. For an overview of different approaches to the relationship between theology and practice, see Ward, *Introducing Practice*.

53. "Convictional theology" has been inspired by the work an American Baptist theologian, James William McClendon. See especially his *Ethics*, 23, and McClendon and Smith, *Convictions*.

the story of the church so far clearly shows the need for a continuing conversion, both personal and communal.

The rest of this book, then, explores the reasons and the paths for such a conversion in relation to the challenge presented by the rise of singleness, in contemporary society and the church itself. Yet although singleness confronts our inherited attitudes toward marriage and the nuclear family, this should not be a cause for fear of further damage to the crumbling patterns of modern family life. Paradoxically, the more we focus exclusively on the family—the nuclear family—the more self-isolated and weaker it becomes. In fact, the life and health of Christian marriages and families depends on the life and health of the believing community as a whole—including its singles.

2

Back to the Roots

From the Old Testament to Jesus

Biblical Family Values—or Old Testament Family Values?

> To attempt to describe the family in the Old Testament
> in one essay is to attempt the impossible.[1]

The discussion of marriage, family, and singleness in the Christian context often turns to the Bible: "What does the Bible say about singleness (or marriage, or family)?" Or, "What are the biblical family values?" In the minds of those appealing to the Bible for family values, the picture of what those values are may seem straightforward. And yet it is anything but—largely because what we assume as "family" today is very different from how family looked in biblical times. Let us start with the Old Testament.

First of all, there is no word in the Scriptures for what we today think of as "family." Instead, there are two closely related concepts: *household* and *kin*. The first refers to a place which functions both as a home and a business, and the second is about relationship networks based on blood and marriage. We will look at both of these aspects below, but at this point it is important to note that in biblical times, "the core or nuclear family existed at the intersection of these two realities, not, as it is seen today, as a freestanding social and residential unit."[2]

---

1. Rogerson, "Family and Structures of Grace," 25.
2. Ruether, *Christianity and the Making of the Modern Family*, 13.

Secondly, if one wishes to talk about "biblical family values" or perhaps a "biblical family model," one would need to select from a whole range of value sets and models. One model, for example, is Adam and Eve; another is Abram, Sarai, and Hagar; yet another is Solomon and his wives and concubines. Some of the family stories include what we today would clearly class as an abuse of children or of women, and there is plenty of deceit, betrayal, and murder. (Check, for instance, such stories as Gen 4:1–16; Judg 19; or 2 Sam 11—certainly not passages for some light reading.) If there is one common aspect to all of these families, it is that in the Old Testament world, with very few exceptions, marriage—polygamous or monogamous, to a wife or to a concubine—was simply assumed.

For women, never marrying was nothing short of a tragedy: a woman's purpose (and the measure of her worth) was in giving successful births to children (preferably boys). Unmarried men were also few, and their singleness had to do either with a personal misfortune or an exceptional calling of God. Castration was forbidden for the Israelites, but the Old Testament mentions eunuchs serving as officers or courtiers. Despised for having no "manhood" and viewed as impaired, they were excluded from the community of Israel and its public worship (Deut 23:1) and would have likely been foreigners. Another exception would be extraordinary prophetic figures. An example of such is the prophet Jeremiah, who is commanded not to marry and to remain childless as a prophetic sign of the doom awaiting Israel (Jer 16). The Lord also commands Jeremiah not to attend funerals or weddings. Assuring ridicule and shame for Jeremiah personally, he was a prophetic picture of the terrible judgement awaiting the wayward people of God.[3] The very extraordinariness of Jeremiah's unmarried situation is a reflection of how fundamental marriage and children were for the Jewish understanding of a good and godly life.

The purpose of biblical marriages was the continuation of the family line through the sons. A later Talmudic writer put it this way: "He who does not engage in procreation of the human race is as though he sheds human blood."[4] Family name mattered a great deal in the culture of shame and honor, and it lived on through its descendants, making it a crucial piece of one's identity.[5] In fact, marriage was necessary precisely *because* it was the vehicle for producing heirs. In that sense, it was not the lack of marriage as such that was to be grieved, but childlessness. This also helps to understand polygamy as a way of addressing the problem of childlessness.

3. Craigie et al., *Jeremiah 1–25*, 219.

4. Quoted in Nathan, *Family*, 39.

5. Mackin, "Primitive Christian Understanding," 23.

It is not surprising, therefore, that a number of Old Testament stories are centered around the lack of children—a source of deep shame and anguish for the wives who found themselves barren. Hagar, a slave, appears in the lives of Abram and Sarai in order to produce an heir for Abram's line (Gen 16). Tamar, the widow of Er, is to be married to Er's brother, and after his death expects to marry the remaining brother—all in order to produce an heir for her first husband. When this last marriage does not happen, Tamar eventually resorts to seducing her father-in-law, Judah, in order to get pregnant (Gen 38). Hannah, one of the wives of Elkanah, is tormented by her barrenness, and in deep distress presents herself to God (1 Sam 1). In the world of the Old Testament, marriage, family, and children are an essential aspect of life, and a key element of how God's will is carried out.

Patriarchy and Blood Links

> The family in ancient Israel . . . was far more advantageous to men than to women.[6]

Family in biblical times was a highly patriarchal structure. "The family—of the 'father's house'—was the strongest source of identity and inclusion for the Israelite person," notes theological ethicist Lisa Sowle Cahill.[7] The phrase "the father's house" (*bet 'av* in Hebrew) is important here: the "father"—a patriarch—would be the head and the center of this world which would include wives, descendants, slaves, and other property. Together with all the descendants, extending up to four or even five generations, such a family could be as large as 100 persons.[8] The value of the individual was always understood in terms of the family they belonged to. For women, it had special implications, as the virginity of the unmarried daughters and sexual loyalty of the wives was crucial for maintaining the honor of the family.

A key feature of ancient family arrangements was the importance of the blood links. A son would always be expected to be wholly loyal to his father—the patriarch of the house.[9] But the strongest emotional attachment would typically be that of a son and his mother, and it was by far more significant than that of a husband and his wife (or wives).[10] Bonds between siblings were

6. Rogerson, "Family and Structures of Grace," 41.

7. Cahill, "Christian Social Perspective," 162–63.

8. For a helpful description of Jewish families in biblical times, see Rogerson, "Family and Structures of Grace."

9. Moxnes, "What Is Family?," 34.

10. Bernabé, "Of Eunuchs," 131.

also highly treasured—especially relationships with those who shared the same mother as well as the father. Indeed, the epitome of a family tragedy was the rupture of relationships between brothers.[11] In this light, many of the Old Testament stories of strife among siblings are a reflection of the world marred by sin, a world in which one is no longer one's brother's keeper (Gen 4:9–10). Brotherly ties were also the reason for providing economic relief to family members in need. In another important sense, however, the same "brother-ethic" was to be extended to every Israelite. John Rogerson, a biblical scholar, refers to such an ethic as a "structure of grace": "Any needy Israelite, regardless of family or genealogy, has a claim upon his more prosperous neighbor, a claim grounded in the fact that the people as a whole are called by God to be a holy people."[12] As we will see later, such a "structure of grace" was to be adopted by the church of Jesus, with every believer being treated as a sister or brother.

Marriage in the Old Testament can really only be understood in the context of these patriarchal blood links. It was a covenant—not between two people, but between two usually already related families. Although we love our Bible love stories like Isaac and Rebekah, it is important to bear in mind that the preferences of the spouses-to-be, though not necessarily ignored, certainly did not play the major role in most cases. So much more was at stake than just two people's desire for each other: this was about extending the power of one's family and consolidating its property. It is for that reason that desiring someone else's wife could be compared to desiring someone else's animals or any other property (Exod 20:17).

Celibates for the End of Times

> I was informed that one, whose name was Banus, lived in the desert . . . and had no other food than what grew of its own accord, and bathed himself in cold water frequently, both by night and by day, in order to preserve his chastity. I imitated him in those things, and continued with him three years.[13]

Although marriage and producing children continued to function as a basic obligation, value, and purpose for most Jews, a new development emerged from around 200 BC. Perhaps many generations feel like they are living in a

11. Hellerman, *When the Church Was a Family*, 48.

12. Rogerson, "Family and Structures of Grace," 38.

13. Josephus, *Life*, 2.

time of crisis and on the verge of the "end," but that was certainly true of that volatile period of the Jewish history. As one oppressive regime or occupant replaced another, the mood in Israel turned intensely apocalyptic. Visions and oracles about the coming of God's Messiah and the end of the world kept turning up, encouraging the people to trust that God would soon deliver victory for Israel over its enemies. Several of the sects that emerged at this time took great interest in sexual abstinence—although for some, only after leaving their already existing spouses and children.[14] Literary fragments point to two of such groups, although little can be said with absolute certainty.

One of them was a community of celibate Jewish mystics based in Egypt, called the Therapeutae. What is quite noteworthy is that women were regarded as equals among the Therapeutae, and were included in the community activities, such as meditation and the study of Scriptures. Their contemporary, Jewish philosopher Philo, describes these women as mostly "aged virgins who have maintained their purity not under constraint . . . but voluntarily through their zealous desire for wisdom. Eager to enjoy intimacy with her, they have been unconcerned with the pleasures of the body, desiring a progeny not mortal but immortal."[15] The men may well have been married at some point of their lives, but joining this community they would "have given up possession of their property, with nothing further to entice them . . . abandoning brothers, children, wives, parents, numerous kin, dear companions, the fatherlands in which they were born and reared."[16]

The other sect was the Essenes, scattered throughout the Judean villages. (The community at Qumran, of the Dead Sea Scrolls fame, may have been one of such groups, although scholars continue to debate the matter.) In contrast to the Therapeutae, the Essenes included only men. Jewish priest and historian Josephus reported some of them to "neglect wedlock, but choose out other persons' children, while they are pliable, and fit for learning, and esteem them to be of their kindred, and form them according to their own manners. They do not absolutely deny the fitness of marriage, and the succession of mankind thereby continued; but they guard against the lascivious behavior of women, and are persuaded that none of them preserve their fidelity to one man."[17]

The sources on the Essenes are conflicting, so we do not really know how widely celibacy was practiced amongst different branches of the sect. However, some members were certainly celibate, and for others, their marital activity would have been regularly restricted due to the Essene focus on ritual

14. Deming, *Paul on Marriage*, 95.

15. Philo, *Contempl.* 68.

16. Philo, *Contempl.* 18.

17. Josephus, *J.W.* 2.8.2.

purity. Arising particularly from the holiness rules described in the book of
Leviticus, sexual abstinence was required in preparation for religious service,
holy warfare, and by implication other holy occasions. (See also Exod 19:15,
where Moses commands the people not to go "near a woman" in preparation
for the Lord's visitation.) Regarding the temple priests as corrupt and temple
services as illegitimate, the Essenes "saw themselves as a living sanctuary . . .
where they offered up the heave-offering of prayer and a perfect conduct as
a pleasing sacrifice. God has chosen them as living stones for his house."[18] In
other words, living in the spirit of preparing for the atonement of Israel and
for God's coming judgement of the world would have likely made celibacy a
"practical necessity."[19]

In stark contrast to the dominant Jewish culture, these people were willing to abandon their natural families for the sake of a new spiritual reality.[20]
Something was in the air, and it was likely not limited to the Essenes: expecting an overhaul of the world order, various "ascetic figures . . . continued
to emerge from the desert to preach repentance to the nearby cities."[21] The
appearance of John the Baptist and Jesus takes place within this background.

Jesus and His New Family

We regard the good news of new life in Jesus as a truly family-
friendly message. But Jesus often emphasized precisely the opposite, namely, the gospel's potential to irrevocably undermine
family unity and to divide family members against one another.[22]

Consider these words of Jesus: "Who are my mother and my brothers? . . .
Whoever does the will of God is my brother and sister and mother" (Mark
3:33, 35). Or even, "Whoever comes to me and does not hate father and mother, wife and children, brothers and sisters, yes, and even life itself, cannot be
my disciple" (Luke 14:26). Finally, anyone considering following Jesus would
have had to take heed of this warning: "For I have come to set a man against
his father, and a daughter against her mother, and a daughter-in-law against
her mother-in-law; and one's foes will be members of one's own household"
(Matt 10:35–36).

18. Betz, "Essenes," 450.

19. Baumgarten, "Celibacy," 124.

20. Betz, "Essenes," 449.

21. Brown, *Body and Society*, 40.

22. Hellerman, *When the Church Was a Family*, 54.

Read with fresh eyes, such words strike one as "anti-family"—and, as we shall see later, it was one of the accusations thrown at the early churches by their contemporaries. The new community of Jesus was to supersede and redefine all previous group loyalties for the sake of the new creation called the kingdom of God. However, although this was a truly countercultural redefinition of marriage and family bonds, we should also note that the signs of this subversion were already present in the Old Testament. While marriage and procreation play a central role in its stories, it also contains a promise that one day, faithful eunuchs will be fully included in the community of God's people, being given "a monument and a name better than sons and daughters" (Isa 56:5). If one has ears to hear, the Hebrew Scriptures ring with a call to expand the familial boundaries, to care for all the Israelites, and beyond that, for the alien, the widow, and the orphan, looking after the good of "the neighbor" as much as for the good of oneself and one's own kin. In Jesus' teaching, this call is amplified so that it becomes the key element of what it means to seek God and God's presence.

In Jesus' words, his community of faith, and his primary family, would be those who "do the will of my Father" (Matt 12:50). And what a family! Jesus describes them as eunuchs, children, and slaves—in other words, the unimportant, or even disgraceful, members of society.[23] Anyone could join; everyone was to be welcome as a new sister or brother, whatever their economic or social status.

Two fishermen, James and John, sons of Zebedee, are described leaving their father and their fishing boat in order to travel with Jesus and see the kingdom of God drawing near (Matt 4:21–22). The symbolism of leaving a father behind can be easily missed by a contemporary reader, but, as we have already seen, in the culture of the time, one's father would continue to play a central role throughout one's life. Thus their act of leaving one's father carried a much more significant—and shocking—message than we may imagine.[24]

James and John are by far no exceptions. Jesus said as much: an aspiring disciple might expect having to leave behind father, mother, brothers, sisters, wife, children, house, or fields (Matt 19:27–30; Mark 10:28–31; Luke 18:28–30). Notice that "fields" and "houses" go together with the people the disciple leaves behind: a reminder that one's livelihood in the traditional society of biblical Palestine was inconceivable apart from one's family and household. What the disciples forsake, therefore, is not simply family as an "emotional

---

23. Matt 19:12–15; 20:26–27. Cf. Osiek and Balch, *Families in the New Testament World*, 133–34.

24. Moxnes, "What Is Family?," 37.

unit," to use contemporary language, but first and foremost, a socio-economic structure and its relationships.[25]

Yet the prospect of having to abandon one's own relationships and economic base is accompanied by a promise. There is no one, says Jesus, who would leave their old support network and not receive, already in this life, "a hundredfold" (or in Luke's language, "very much more"). The promise of "a hundredfold" tells us that Jesus is not after destroying human relationships or economic and social wellbeing, but rather reimagining these. One's family and household was a sizeable structure already, so how many more houses will the disciples be welcomed into on their missionary journeys or fleeing from persecution, how many fields will be generously shared for producing food, and how many more new mothers, brothers, sisters, and children will they acquire in this new family![26]

Curiously, in this new "hundredfold" family, there is no patriarch—only houses, brothers and sisters, mothers and children, and fields (and also persecutions: Mark 10:29–30).[27] Given that fathers were the embodiment of patriarchal family structure, such an intentional exclusion of the most important traditional family member from the list of Jesus' new family would have been scandalously obvious. Over against this fatherly image, the new family of Jesus is to have only one Father—"the one in heaven" (Matt 23:9).

Such a radical reinterpretation of human bonds must be read in the light of Jesus' teaching about the nature of the kingdom of God which is already present, even if not yet in its fullness. What has been "normal," such as eating, drinking, marrying, and being given in marriage, is now interrupted by the dawn of the new era of the kingdom (Matt 24:37–39; Luke 17:26–27, 30). Theologians sometimes describe the focus on this ultimate reality of the kingdom as *eschatological*—arising from "the sense that history had reached a turning-point, even (in some sense) come to an end."[28] The promise and the signs of this new reality, inaugurated with Jesus being raised from the dead, means a radical change in viewing both marriage and singleness.[29]

25. Moxnes, "What Is Family?," 23.

26. Among things and persons which may need to be left for the sake of the kingdom, the Gospel of Luke includes "wife"—but no new wives, and certainly not hundredfold, are promised in return.

27. Schüssler Fiorenza, *In Memory of Her*, 1478.

28. Barton, "Marriage, Family, the Bible and the Gospel," 166.

29. Clapp, *Families at the Crossroads*, 89.

Jesus on Marriage and Singleness

> It is likely that while Jesus' teaching on marriage was a shock, his teaching on singleness would have seemed even more stunning.[30]

Jesus' teaching on marriage, as well as abstaining from marriage, was at the core of the "hard words" which many of his listeners found just too difficult to stomach. For one, while being accused of spending his time in the company of prostitutes and other kinds of shady characters, he appears to have been a stickler for an already existing marriage.[31] In Matt 19:3–12, the Pharisees throw Jesus a "hot potato"—a question they are fiercely debating amongst themselves.[32] What grounds for divorcing one's wife are legitimate? Jesus surprises the Pharisees by insisting that in God's presence, where the human hardness of the heart has been melted, there is to be no divorcing one's wife, except for her unfaithfulness. In fact, in the Gospels of Mark (10:11) and Luke (16:18), not even unfaithfulness serves as legitimate grounds for divorce and remarriage.

Lest we, like the Pharisees, get hung up on the conditions upon which divorce is "legit," we need to keep in mind the lopsided structure of marriage in Jewish Palestine. While the men could spend their time clarifying under which conditions they could initiate a divorce from their wife, the Jewish women did not have such an option. In the event of divorce, the woman was always the loser. The threat of divorce was especially acute in the case of woman's barrenness, but she could be discarded at any point of her life, perhaps for such a minor "offence" as bad cooking, or simply because the husband's eyes had moved onto another woman.

When Jesus says that one can't divorce one's wife, his own disciples are baffled: if marriage is to be "for forever," then, from the perspective of a man, it is better not to marry at all! Yet it is almost certainly uttered in disbelief: of course men are expected to marry. Incredibly, Jesus responds in all seriousness: indeed, in the new age of the kingdom of heaven, remaining unmarried—living as a "eunuch"—can be a real and commendable option. Jesus describes three different kinds of eunuchs: some who are born "this way"; some who are single because of what has been done to them; and those who have chosen it "for the sake of the kingdom of heaven," prefiguring the ordering of relationships as they will be in the kingdom of God. And let's bear in

30. Witherington, *Matthew*, 364.

31. It is worth noting, however, that some other rabbis of Jesus' time held similar views. Nathan, *Family*, 40.

32. Lutz, *Matthew 8–20*, 488–89.

mind that a "eunuch" was not exactly a flattering description. Pitied, laughed at, detested, or slighted, they would not be mentioned favorably, even less so in the same breath as "the kingdom of heaven."[33] It would seem that Jesus—by all accounts himself an unmarried man—once again may have picked up and subverted a derogatory title thrown at him.[34]

Thus, while insisting on total commitment within marriage, Jesus also normalizes—more than that, celebrates—the unmarried state. Jesus proclaims the fulfillment of the promise recorded in Isaiah: those without children (and therefore without future), those derided and rejected, are drawn into the very center of the kingdom community.[35] In fact, it is more than a matter of inclusion and justice. Theologian Stanley Hauwerwas puts it this way: "Followers of Jesus do not need to marry or have children to be followers of Jesus, because the kingdom does not grow by biological ascription, but through witness and conversion."[36] Jesus reinterprets the point of marriage in the light of the bigger story of God's kingdom, and presents an unmarried state as something which can be willingly embraced.

Yet one of the most puzzling stories, reported in Matthew, Mark, and Luke, is Jesus' exchange with the Sadducees—the religious and political Jewish elite of the time—in which Jesus says that after the resurrection of all the faithful, they will neither marry nor be given in marriage, but will be "like angels in heaven" (e.g., Mark 12:25). This saying appears in response to the trap which the Sadducees have set up for Jesus, based on the following question: who will be married to whom, if there is such a thing as the resurrection from the dead at the end of time? Or to put it more bluntly, who will "own" a childless woman who had been serially married to seven brothers during her lifetime?[37]

Here is how Luke records Jesus' response: "Those who belong to this age marry and are given in marriage; but those who are considered worthy of a place in that age and in the resurrection from the dead neither marry nor are given in marriage. Indeed they cannot die anymore, because they are like angels and are children of God, being children of the resurrection" (Luke 20:34b–36).

Many contemporary Bible readers are likely to find this to be quite a perplexing, if not upsetting, passage. In fact, if life here on earth is one's only chance to experience marriage, then perhaps it is best to make sure one does not "miss out"? And here's the rub: as we shall see later, our understanding of

33. Davies and Allison, *Matthew*, 25.

34. Baltensweiler, "Eunuch," 561.

35. Isa 56:3–5. See also 54:1–3 for the promise given to a barren woman.

36. Hauerwas, *Matthew*, 306.

37. Myers et al., *"Say to this Mountain,"* 163.

happiness is so tightly connected to the idea of coupledom that couple-less idea of heaven just isn't palatable. We simply cannot fathom anything "even better" than marriage, for the latter has become an epitome of personal happiness. But I am getting ahead of myself.

At the very least, this passage suggests transformed relationships where people are neither owned nor passed around if they fail the fertility test. The hypothetical woman from the Sadducees' story need not worry as to whom she will be assigned to in the life to come. The patriarchal arrangement which her marriages reflected will be no more. There will be no death, and therefore no need to continue family name through giving birth.[38]

Jesus as the Key for Interpreting the Scriptures

The words of the text have to be interpreted in the light
of the Living Word, who is Jesus Christ.[39]

What are we to do with this daring vision for the ordering of human relationships? The structures and patterns of human relationships in the Jewish Palestine of Jesus' times may seem so different from our environment today. And even where we recognize similarities and parallels, we may struggle to see how exactly they apply to the life in the twenty-first century. But, in the words of biblical scholar Stephen Barton, "to read [the Bible] wisely, you often have to go below the surface level and ask, What's the bigger picture, and how does that bigger picture allow the text still to speak today? This means that the Bible has to be interpreted in the light of the gospel, for the gospel is the bigger picture."[40] If that is the case, then Jesus' words about marriage and singleness, however radical they may sound, somehow need to be at the core of thinking about singleness and marriage today.

It is hard to argue against the fact that some of the sayings of Jesus are truly shocking, at least at a surface reading. Yet time and again, Jesus responds compassionately to the pleas of those who are begging him to heal their family member: the dying daughter of a synagogue leader (Mark 5:21–43), the sick son of a royal official (John 4:46–54), or the mother-in-law of one of Jesus' closest disciples, Peter (Luke 4:38–39). Here we find a reminder that Jesus' reaction to family structures was not a rejection of human love and care for those nearest and dearest. It is particularly evident in Jesus' responses to the

38. Green, *Gospel of Luke*, 721.
39. Barton, "Marriage, Family, the Bible and the Gospel," 165.
40. Barton, "Marriage, Family, the Bible and the Gospel," 165.

requests to help a sick or dying child. In a society in which children did not carry a value in and of themselves, Jesus reacts to the parental distress with compassion and generosity.[41]

We may also recall the bond between Jesus and his mother, especially as portrayed in the Gospel of John. She launches his ministry at the wedding at Cana, where God's glory is revealed on an occasion of celebrating a marriage of two people (2:3–5). She is present under the cross as he is dying, along with Jesus' aunt (19:25–27). There, Jesus also fulfills his duty as a son by making sure Mary is taken care of after he is gone (presumably because Mary is a widow at this point), by asking "the disciple whom he loved" to adopt her.

However, these stories need to be kept in tension with a reminder that Jesus' own family considers him to be demon-possessed and seeks to protect their family honor by removing him from public ministry (Mark 3:21–35). Jesus' own experience is a precursor of what will happen to his followers: in his own words, "brother will betray brother to death, and a father his child, and children will rise against parents and have them put to death; and you will be hated by all because of my name" (Matt 10:21–22).

Such a teaching defied, and continues to defy, the deeply cherished order of things considered to be the best for the human society. The kingdom of God may be compared to a wedding feast (Matt 22:2), but it is not a wedding as we know it: rather, it is the celebration of a new family born of God. We may also take note of Jesus' parable of the great banquet (Luke 14:15–24) in which one of the excuses for not coming to the dinner is being recently married. Marriage need not preclude participating in the kingdom of God; but perhaps it is also a warning that marriage might become an excuse for not responding to the call of Jesus.

Jesus and the Other Unmarrieds

> In the view of the fact that ancient Judaism seems to have regarded it as a religious obligation for a man to marry and raise a family, it is startling that three of the best-known Jews of the first century C.E. appear to have been unmarried—three Jews, moreover, who were prominent in connection with the beginnings of the Christian movement: John the Baptist (forerunner), Jesus (founder), and Paul . . . (a chief apostle).[42]

41. Cahill, "Christian Social Perspective," 165.
42. McArthur, "Celibacy in Judaism," 163.

Jesus is presented to us in the Gospels without a hint of a wife or children—an unusual circumstance given that most Jewish men would have been married at an early age. At the same time, refraining from sex was a sign of prophetic ministry and a condition for participating in sacred service: we have seen this already in the example of the Essenes and the Therapeutae.[43] Yet it is still astounding how many apparently unmarried people there seem to be associated with Jesus and his movement. This is particularly true of women, who range from patrons to widows to prostitutes. In fact, "not a single woman with whom Jesus speaks in the gospels is explicitly represented as married. . . . This lack of marital identifiers tends to be true for men as well; it might reflect the actual marital status of Jesus' followers or merely the disinterest of the evangelists (or even both)."[44]

Jesus' public ministry is enabled by a number of unattached women, among whom the most known, no doubt, is Mary Magdalene. Together with other women who had been healed by Jesus, she follows him and his disciples—a scandalous thing to do for a woman—and supports them out of her own resources (Luke 8:1–3).[45] Although details about her in the Gospels are scarce, she looms large in the Christian tradition and has continued to fascinate people's imaginations ever since. Just like Susanna, mentioned in the same verse, she is introduced without any reference to a husband, thereby making it all but certain that she was not married: an anomaly in a culture which would have expected women to be married (and hopefully hard at work in producing progeny) at a very early age.[46] However, Mary's unmarried state may be explained by the fact that Luke introduces her as the one "from whom seven demons had gone out." The label of demon possession carried with itself a stigma and the likelihood of being shunned; so it is conceivable that after being healed of her affliction, Mary and others like her identified with Jesus and his followers as their new family.[47]

Another recognizable group are three siblings: Mary, Martha, and Lazarus. The two sisters are particularly interesting. In Luke 10:38–42, they are presented as two independent women: "no hint of a brother, much less

43. McArthur, "Celibacy in Judaism," 166–67; 171–73.

44. Kraemer and D'Angelo, *Women and Christian Origins*, 40.

45. "It was not uncommon for women to support rabbis and their disciples out of their own money, property, or foodstuffs. But for her to leave home and travel with a rabbi was not only unheard of, it was scandalous." Witherington, "On the Road," 135.

46. Conversely, the third woman mentioned in the same verse, Joanna, is clearly identified as "the wife of Chuza."

47. Green, *Gospel of Luke*, 318.

a father or a husband, disturbs this autonomous female household."[48] Just as scandalously as Mary Magdalene and other women who were freely traveling with Jesus and his disciplines, Martha (quite likely "a patroness in comfortable circumstances"[49]) welcomes Jesus (a man!) into her home. Even in John 11–12, where Lazarus appears alongside the two sisters, he is not at the center of the stage.[50] We cannot say for sure whether all three of them would have shared the same house; it could be that they simply lived in the same village. Luke's recounting of Jesus visiting Martha and Mary's home would suggest this being the case, as Lazarus—who would have otherwise been the head of the house—is not mentioned. If so, the most probable scenario would have been that Lazarus had his own house and family, and Mary and Martha would be "probably . . . two unmarried sisters sharing the same household."[51] Notably, however, when Lazarus gets seriously ill, it is his sisters—not wife—who call for Jesus.[52] Whichever the case, they are an illustration of how close the sibling bonds were in the culture of Jesus' time.

Yet another important group of unmarried people for whom Jesus has a lot of time is the widows, who often feature in Jesus' life and parables as tireless and faithful participants of the kingdom. One of the stories from Jesus' infancy describes the prophetess Anna, who, very unusually, seems to have been a widow from a young age without remarrying (Luke 2:36–38), a testimony to "the single woman's possibility of single-mindedness, of living completely for God, without any interference from other obligations."[53] Jesus' own mother, Mary, is commonly believed to be a widow by the Christian tradition, given the disappearance of any record of Joseph from the Scripture after Jesus' infancy and childhood stories.

Jesus raises the only son of a widow at Nain (Luke 7:11–17) and tells a story of a persistent widow who prevails upon an unjust judge as a reminder of the justness of God (Luke 18:1–8). Technically, a "genuine" widow was not simply a woman whose husband has died, but the one who had no adult male relative (a father, a grown-up son, or the deceased husband's brother) willing or able to take care of her. Without legal, social, and economic protection, with no one to speak up for her, she could be extremely vulnerable, and in Scriptures she is often a symbol of the poor and the oppressed.

48. Alexander, "Sisters in Adversity," 198.

49. Seim, *Double Message*, 99.

50. Seim, *Double Message*, 97.

51. Aasgaard, '*My Beloved Brothers*,' 66.

52. Aasgaard, '*My Beloved Brothers*,' 65.

53. Seim, *Double Message*, 244.

In some circumstances, however, being a widow meant considerably greater independence compared to a young virgin or a married woman, whose lot was determined by her male relatives. If there were financial resources available for her use, a widow actually had a choice whether to marry again or stay single (especially if she already had children). This, as we will see, soon became an important point of consideration for the first churches.

Our next chapter will take us to this next episode in the story of the Christian church. Reflecting a radical shift from the assumption of marriage as a norm and children as an essential aspect of a good and godly life, these new communities of disciples sought to make sense of Jesus' teaching on singleness and marriage in the context of the Jewish culture and the Roman Empire.

3

Life in the New Family

Christian Witness in the New Testament World

Family in the Greco-Roman World

> [The Roman] marriage was, fundamentally, a partnership for the
> purposes of reproduction. . . . Once conception of legitimate chil-
> dren had taken place, the contract could be revoked by death or
> divorce without damage to the legitimacy of the offspring.[1]

By the beginning of the Christian era, Israel was part of an enormous cosmopolitan empire. Jews of different social classes could be found living in
and traveling everywhere, including the empire's center, Rome. Of course, the
culture of the Roman Empire was not a "Roman" culture as such—for several
centuries already it had been heavily formed by Greek culture—but the latter
was now being shaped by the "highly sophisticated forms of propaganda" run
by the Romans.[2]

In Palestine, the Jewish and gentile worlds coexisted and interacted in
a variety of ways. The life of the Jewish aristocracy in Palestine's urban areas
would have been not too dissimilar to that of the Roman families. Poorer in-
habitants of the towns and cities would have tried to recreate the feel of their
ancestral village, making sure that an extended family lived together in close
proximity.[3] But even in the villages, more sheltered from the Greco-Roman

1. Cooper, *Fall*, 149.
2. Winter, *Roman Wives*, 33.
3. Ruether, *Christianity and the Making of the Modern Family*, 18.

culture, one was never too far from the signs and expressions of the imperial world. Greek-speaking urban centers with their baths, theaters, and temples were only a short journey away from traditional Jewish settlements. Trade routes brought people from all over, and devout Jews would make pilgrimages to Jerusalem, mingling there with travelers from foreign lands and cultures.

The movement of the early followers of Jesus soon started spreading across the empire, not only among the cosmopolitan Jews but also, increasingly, among the non-Jewish converts to the Way, particularly through the ministry and missionary travels of the apostle Paul and his coworkers. Before too long, believers of Jewish background were a minority among those who pledged their allegiance to Jesus of Nazareth.

What kind of families and households did these new believers come from? The empire was vast, so there would have been many regional and class differences. However, we can start with a few general observations. Marriage as a legal status was by itself a privilege not necessarily available to everyone, and cohabiting was a well-established practice for those who could not or would not legally marry. Marriage was not permitted, for example, between a man and a slave or a freed slave, a prostitute, or an actress.[4] A widower might have taken a concubine instead of a new wife because he did not want to break up the inheritance.[5] And then there were those who considered marriage and family a burden precluding them from pursuing more worthy things, such as philosophy: "Look at me. . . . I have neither wife nor children, no miserable governor's mansion, but only earth, and sky, and one rough cloak. Yet what do I lack? Am I not free from pain and fear, am I not free?"[6] Cicero reportedly said that "he could not possibly devote himself to a wife and to philosophy."[7]

Marriages were monogamous, at least in the sense that a man would have only one wife at a time. But extramarital relationships were frequent, and prostitution was widespread. Divorce was also common and quite easily available (for either husband or wife, which was in contrast to Jewish law where it was only the man's prerogative).[8] Although marriage was first and foremost a contract between two families, it was supposed to be fulfilled in perfect harmony, or concordia. Conversely, once such harmony, or the desire to maintain marriage, was gone, divorce, or at least separation, was an obvious solution.[9]

---

4. Wiesner-Hanks, *Christianity and Sexuality*, 26.

5. Dixon, *Roman Family*, 93.

6. Epictetus, *Diatr.* 3.22.45–48.

7. Jerome, *Jov.* 1.48.

8. Ferguson, *Backgrounds*, 69.

9. Nathan, *Family*, 17; Wiesner-Hanks, *Christianity and Sexuality*, 26.

The Roman household was an economic unit consisting of all sorts of people who were family in the Roman understanding: the husband, wife, dependent children (or stepchildren), adult sons and their wives, other relatives, apprentices, lodgers, and slaves. Basic education and training took place there, as did religious activities such as commemorating the dead relatives by gathering at the burial place to share a meal and a ritual offering. At the center of it all was the legal head of the family known as the *paterfamilias*—typically a man, although in certain cases it could also be a woman.[10] Other family members were under *paterfamilias'* legal power. Depending on legal variations, the children could remain subject to the same family head even after they themselves were married and established their own households.[11] The children produced by the family slaves were the property of their masters, even if the parent was freed, and cohabiting slaves could be separated and sold at the whim of the one who legally owned them.

The position of wives, however, was in a state of flux. In the first century CE, Roman women started acquiring greater financial and public freedoms—a cause for great concern to some Romans bemoaning the "decline in family life."[12] Some women were now joining their husbands at the public banquets, and becoming much more visible.[13] A "new type" of woman was emerging among the elite: such women both dressed and behaved provocatively, and at times led promiscuous lives.[14] Perhaps most significantly, more and more women followed a new legal custom of not transferring from their original family and the authority of their father when they got married. Even while playing a key role in their husbands' households, they would technically be outside the husband's authority, thereby keeping much greater social and economic independence.[15]

10. Osiek et al., *Woman's Place*, 256.7.

11. Ferguson, *Backgrounds*, 67.

12. Aasgaard, *"My Beloved Brothers,"* 57–59.

13. Osiek et al., *Woman's Place*, 3.

14. Instructions to Christian women in 1 Corinthians and 1 Timothy should be read keeping this development in mind. Winter, *Roman Wives*.

15. LaFosse, "Women, Children and House Churches," 388; Cooper, *Fall*, 146.

We Want You Married and Making Babies:
Imperial Marriage Laws

> [Emperor Augustus] assessed heavier taxes on unmarried men
> and women without husbands, and by contrast offered awards for
> marriage and childbearing.[16]

Although numerous, Roman families lived in the constant shadow of death. Only half of the children would reach adulthood, a woman was not guaranteed to survive childbirth, and life expectancy was shorter than in the poorest corner of the world today. Keeping the number of childbirths up was one of the concerns of the political elite.

Just around the time Jesus was born, Emperor Augustus issued two pieces of legislation aimed at addressing the problem of insufficient population growth and the concern about sliding family values. The legislation required all female citizens (except Vestal Virgins) between the age of twenty and fifty, and every male citizen between the age of twenty-five and sixty, to be married. The childless incurred penalties, and bachelors faced restrictions applied to the inheritance which they could claim.[17] Widows and divorced women had a limited time to remarry after the divorce or the death of their husband. Both the rewards and the penalties were first of all directed at the leading classes, but the rhetoric and the incentives went wider, such as rewards given to freed slaves for producing children.[18]

The reasons for this legislation may have been pragmatic, but Emperor Augustus dressed his action in moral terms: this was about restoring Rome's previous greatness.[19] Certainly enough Romans thought that family standards were slipping.[20] Further pressure was applied when the imperial marriage laws turned out to be quite ineffective in increasing the birth rate. The Emperor "mounted a demonstration of sorts by appearing in public with his grandchildren, in effect presenting a counter-example to errant citizens. He also harangued recalcitrant upper-class bachelors and praised married men in speeches."[21] The image of a good traditional household served as a symbol

---

16. Roman statesman and historian Dio Cassius, *Hist. Rom.* 54.16.1–2, quoted in Winter, *Roman Wives*, 49.

17. Ferguson, *Backgrounds*, 69.

18. Reed, "Paul on Marriage and Singleness," 52.

19. Dixon, *Roman Family*, 79.

20. Aasgaard, 'My Beloved Brothers,' 57–58.

21. Dixon, *Roman Family*, 80.

of the stability of the society; metaphorically, the emperor himself was the *paterfamilias* of the family that was the Roman Empire.[22]

The return to "the imagined morality of the Roman past" proved to be complicated, even when incentives and pressure were applied.[23] Loopholes in the legislation could be used by women who had given birth to a sufficient number of children and had adequate finances: after their divorce or widowing, they could be free from the legal guardianship and able to conduct their business independently.[24] If a widow was over fifty years old, past her childbearing age, she may have wanted to preserve the image of a faithful wife who was married only to her one husband during her lifetime—an ideal which existed alongside and in tension with Augustan marriage laws.[25] This trend enabled some women to become the heads of their own households. It is quite likely to have been the case of Lydia, an independent businesswoman who dyed purple, and whose whole household was baptized as a response to Paul's preaching (Acts 16:14–15).[26]

If a woman did marry, her primary duty as a wife would have been the production of children. Given the likelihood of a child's death before they reached the adulthood, she could expect to give birth multiple times. Those who could not have children but had the means, could adopt.[27] It did not make sense to raise more than one daughter, as she would need a dowry for her marriage.[28] In fact, most families limited their children to one or two, some resorting to abortions or leaving "spare" babies out in the street to die. This would be particularly common if the child was seen to have physical or mental defects, but in general, the head of the family could decide to reject the baby for whatever reason, and it was quite usual for the girls to be abandoned. In the words of one first-century Egyptian husband's letter to his pregnant wife, "If you bear a child and it is male, let it be; if it is female, cast it out."[29]

22. LaFosse, "Women, Children and House Churches," 388.

23. Dixon, *Roman Family*, 120.

24. Osiek et al., *Woman's Place*, 3.

25. Nathan, *Family*, 22.

26. Other examples would be Chloe (1 Cor 1:11); Mary, the mother of John Mark (Acts 12:12), and Nympha (Col 4:15). There is a possibility that they were married to unbelieving husbands, but it seems less likely, as female *paterfamilias*, while certainly unusual, were a legal option in the Roman Empire. Cooper, *Fall*, 111–14; LaFosse, "Women, Children and House Churches," 404.

27. Aasgaard, *'My Beloved Brothers,'* 39.

28. Ferguson, *Backgrounds*, 73.

29. Ilarion, *Papyrus Oxyrhynchus* 4.744.

A New Kind of Family:
New Testament Christians as Brothers and Sisters

> Were Christ and his disciples living today, they would undoubt-
> edly be deemed antifamily by many Christians.[30]

It is with this background knowledge and imagination of the context of early
Christians that we now approach some of the key texts in the New Testament.
In the last chapter, we saw the teaching of Jesus presenting two equally striking
threads: radical faithfulness in marriage and radical choice to abstain from
marriage. The same threads can be recognized in the rest of the New Testament, which we will consider with the first century's cosmopolitan and imperial context in mind.

What connects these two threads is, again, the image of the church as
a new family of God, replacing or at least reshaping the "old" families from
which the believers come. The New Testament is peppered with references to
this new family, most commonly expressed in the language of siblingship.[31]
Chances are we are so used to this terminology that we fail to grasp the significance of it. In the world of the time, calling other believers one's "brothers
and sisters" represented a human bond which went deeper than marriage.[32]

Such a relationship was now binding the followers of the One who called
them all—Jews and gentiles—into a foretaste of heavenly reality, a new community under the fatherhood of God. Their inclusion of different cultures and
classes made this an even more scandalous movement: "People who the kinship rules of the Greeks, Romans, and Jews were designed to distinguish from
one another, and to prevent from intermarrying or eating at table together,
now [shared] a common table and spiritual kinship."[33]

The Acts of the Apostles, as well as the Epistles, tell us that early Christianity grew in an urban environment. Because family also functioned as a center
of religious identity and practice, the Christian disruption of this pattern was,
to put it mildly, problematic. Religion was never a personal matter anyway,
and religious aspects were inseparable from everyday family life. It was far
easier if the head of the household converted, but the conversion of individual
women, or (adult) children under the authority of *paterfamilias*, or slaves, was

---

30. Gillis, *World of Their Own Making*, 23.

31. Following Greek language conventions, the literal meaning of the word is "brothers," which in the New Testament is clearly used to mean both brothers and sisters—see,
for instance, Phil 4:1–2. For further reading on the usage of the term, see Trebilco, "Brothers and Sisters."

32. Bartchy, "Undermining Ancient Patriarchy," 68.

33. Ruether, *Christianity and the Making of the Modern Family*, 28.

an insult to the rest of the family. For a number of these new believers, allegiance to the Christian faith must have meant literally leaving one's structure of life and identity and joining an alternative support system—the church. Of course, not all early Christians had to choose between their biological kin and Christian family; the New Testament also indicates the conversion of whole families and households. In such happy cases, they could become new centers for church gatherings and a key element of the church's growth.

The New Testament has relatively little to say regarding the shape of marriage and family life as such in those early Christian years. The most extended reflection on sexual relationships (or otherwise) in the New Testament is found in chapters 5–7 of the first surviving letter of Paul to the Corinthians, and particularly chapter 7, which deals with the question of singleness and marriage. It is to this passage that we turn next.

Paul to the Corinthians: Do What Is Expedient, as Long as It Is in the Lord

"It is better to marry than to burn," St. Paul had said, but he made it sound like a close call.[34]

First Corinthians 7 is a tricky text to read for several reasons. One of them is that this is not a piece of systematic theology on marriage and singleness, in the manner in which the church fathers would soon write about such subjects. Rather, this is an occasional letter written to people in particular circumstances and facing specific issues, with Paul referring to previous exchanges between him and the Corinthian church. Had Paul written on similar matters to the Christians in Judea or even Rome, chances are he would have phrased things differently and made a different sort of argument. In fact, we have a snippet of this: in a brief reference to marriage in his letter to Christians in Rome, Paul completely forgoes any discussion of the possibility of remaining unmarried, and only points out that a widow can certainly marry again (Rom 7:1–3).[35]

Thus, by reading 1 Corinthians, we are eavesdropping on a conversation the beginning of which we have not heard. The difficulty in making sense of this conversation is attested by widely differing scholarly interpretations of chapter 7: anything from Paul the ascetic advocate of celibate life to Paul the defender of marriage and marital sex.[36] This is a good example of how the

34. Hasslett, "Love Supreme."
35. Deming, *Paul on Marriage*, 210–11.
36. Reed, "Paul on Marriage and Singleness," 59.

interpreters' own views of marriage and singleness can influence what they see (or don't) in the biblical text. In fact, the debate starts with the very first verse in chapter 7, as its reading depends on whether "it is well for a man not to touch a woman" is Paul's opening statement, or—perhaps more likely—a quotation from a letter he received from the Corinthian believers.[37]

However, some things are quite clear. First of all, there is an interest among the Corinthian believers in either staying unmarried, or separating, or stopping sexual relations within an existing marriage. Some of this interest might have to do with cultural trends: certain philosophers and doctors popular in Corinth considered sexual abstinence an ideal to live by, and some Corinthians might have found it attractive in their pursuit of a particular kind of body-denying spirituality. ("Spiritual" is a word that appears in 1 Corinthians more than in any other book in the Bible.[38]) Some of the well-to-do widows who were the heads of their own households might have been reluctant to remarry and lose control over managing their own households. Others—men and women—may have wanted "out" of their marriage with an unbelieving spouse given the tensions it was creating.[39]

However, at least some of their interest in unmarried life must have stemmed from the Corinthian believers' embracing of the story of Jesus, his redefinition of family values, and his counter-cultural praise for the "eunuchs for the Kingdom." Paul describes unmarried life in similar terms: there are more important things to be concerned about, namely, "the affairs of the Lord," and marriage can get in the way (7:32–34). This is especially true because "the appointed time has grown short;" "the present form of this world is passing away" (7:29, 31)—notice the same anticipation as in Jesus' teaching, of the Kingdom of God drawing near and already here.

Paul offers his own example of living as an unmarried person who has a "gift" of single living (7:7)—although we do not know whether he was never married (rather unlikely given his upbringing), or (perhaps more probably) was a widower.[40] What we know, however, is that remaining unmarried is Paul's preferred option, which he wishes for others too, as long as they can handle it. Notice that Paul's preference for remaining unmarried is *not* based on abstaining from sex—rather, it is because single life grants one greater

37. For a discussion of these views, see, for example, Deming, *Paul on Marriage*, 107–8.

38. Osiek and Balch, *Families in the New Testament World*, 109. On the medical praise for sexual abstinence, see Soranus, *Soranus' Gynecology*, 30. For an in-depth discussion of the Cynic and Stoic views on marriage, and their echoes in 1 Cor 7, see Deming, *Paul on Marriage*.

39. MacDonald, "Reading 1 Corinthians," 40–41.

40. Thiselton, *First Epistle*, 512–13.

freedom to give undivided attention to the life and the growth of the kingdom of God. As we will see, the emphasis on sexual asceticism which will be read into 1 Corinthians 7 later will change the shape of marriage and singleness significantly, "demanding a choice between sexuality and spirituality."[41] But for Paul, the discussion is not about any particular holiness arising out of sexual abstinence. Instead, it is making decisions about the shape of one's life "on the basis of expediency,"[42] and being free from having to "please" a husband (producing children and managing the household) or wife (providing enough for the whole family and maintaining their social standing).

Let us stop for a moment to take in the effect that Paul's words on singleness must have had. By the time of Paul's writing, Corinth was very much a Roman colony. The cultural climate, as we have already seen, was deeply impacted by the central role of marriage and procreation as the vehicle for the progression of civilized life. "There was no word for 'old maid,'" bachelors were fined for failing to reproduce, and the imperial marriage laws made it clear that men and women of fertile age "should be married as continuously as possible."[43] The vision of a good life that Paul is offering is contrary to both the custom and legislation of the empire.

Paul concedes that not everybody is able to live without marriage and exercise the self-control that singleness requires. In that case, he says, let the people marry (7:9). Even a widow can marry again (although "only in the Lord," that is, only to someone from the new family of God). Personally, however, he thinks she would be better off "if she remains as she is" (7:40). But marriage is a structure of this world which is passing away (7:31; cf. Luke 20:35). Quite frankly, it seems to be no more than a prophylactic against lust: it is not sinful as such, but it is for those who cannot control their desire (7:36).

However, there is another surprising and subversive element in Paul's understanding of marriage, very much at odds with how it was understood both by Jews and the Greco-Roman society. Let us recall that the whole point of marriage, and sex within marriage, was producing children. And yet, strikingly, Paul does not mention children as the reason, or "the point," of sexual activity between spouses. Instead, rather extraordinarily, he talks about intimacy, mutuality, and faithfulness.[44] In contrast to sexual asceticism which will characterize the Christianity of later times, here we have an affirmation of bodily union, reciprocal vulnerability, and mutual responsibility—not only

---

41. Deming, *Paul on Marriage*, 219.

42. Deming, *Paul on Marriage*, 219.

43. Seim, *Double Message*, 192.

44. Osiek and Balch, *Families in the New Testament World*, 118.

for the wife to take care of her husband's bodily needs and desires, but also for the husband to do the same in relation to his wife.

Thus, just like Jesus, Paul seems to take marriage very seriously, in a way that does not fit the Greco-Roman or even the Jewish mold, neither of which saw a great issue in divorce and remarriage. Spouses who are believers are not to separate, and if they do, they should seek reconciliation (10–11). The same is true for someone who has joined the new family of Jesus in Corinth, but whose spouse has not: however easy it would be to obtain divorce, if the unbelieving spouse is willing to stay in the marriage, it should not be broken. Yet "if the unbelieving partner separates, let it be so; in such a case the brother or sister is not bound" (1 Cor 7:15). Whether being "not bound" refers to freedom to leave the marriage, or to remarry, the debate continues,[45] but we can make two conclusions. First, divorce or separation are to be the last resort for those belonging to the family of God. Secondly, the top priority is one's allegiance to Christ and his church: these are more important things than whether one is married or not. This is why Paul is not at all excited to hear of those who are hurrying to change their marital status: "Are you bound to a wife? Do not seek to be free. Are you free from a wife? Do not seek a wife" (7:27). He then finishes the discussion with his advice repeating his order of preference: whoever marries, "does well," but the one who chooses not to marry "will do better" (7:38).

What are we to take from this conversation between Paul and the Corinthian believers? Perhaps the starting point would be not to try to build a whole theology of singleness, marriage, and divorce on the basis of this one passage. Instead, we could seek to absorb the spirit of Paul's words: his feeling that single life is truly valuable because it involves less distress (7:28), less anxiety (7:32), more order and unhindered devotion to the Lord (7:35), and in general can be more "blessed" or "happy" (7:40). Today, such a notion runs against the grain of what is considered to be a "happy" life, both within and outside the church.

However, Paul's description of marriage is also a bold reminder that bodily needs constitute a key aspect of Christian marriage, and that those needs are to be met reciprocally. It also underscores that marriage imposes particular limitations—the need to adapt one's life around the spouse's needs. For that reason, it requires extra work in order to be aligned with the wider life of the family of God's people. As Joseph Hellerman puts it, "Paul's concern in 1 Corinthians 7 was not to ask how singleness fits into God's kingdom plan. Paul was addressing the issue of how marriage fits into His kingdom plan. Single people are already with the program. They are 'concerned about the things of

---

45. Thiselton, *First Epistle*, 534–43.

the Lord' (v. 32). Married people are the ones who need help sorting out their priorities."[46]

"So as to Give the Adversary No Occasion to Revile Us": Towards an Orderly and Harmonious Life

> Imperial culture stood ready to evaluate the respectability of what would be perceived as Christian behavior.[47]

Transforming priorities, however, is a complex task, and that complexity is reflected in the witness of the Scriptures. On the one hand, the radical nature of God's new family was signaled by the sibling language and Paul's order of preference in 1 Cor 7. On the other hand, several other New Testament passages contain instructions for a hierarchical ordering of relationships and mutual responsibilities within a household: wives and husbands, slaves and masters, parents and (adult!) children. Known as "household codes," their form follows that of the domestic codes originating in ancient Greek thought and used by various authors in the Roman times. Instead of the language of disciples as "brothers and sisters," here the dominant image employed is that of the "household of God" (Eph 2:19; 1 Tim 3:15; 1 Pet 4:17).[48]

Notably, in the three versions which follow the classical domestic code structure most closely (Eph 5:21–6:9; Col 3:18–4:1; and 1 Pet 2:18–3:7), there are no instructions for unmarried believers: they are subsumed under the authority of a patriarchal family head. Some other passages elaborate on the guidelines for dealing with the widows in the church: they are to be honored, but only if they are "real widows"—at least sixty years old and having been married only once (1 Tim 5:9). As to younger widows, they are to "marry, bear children, and manage their households" (1 Tim 5:14). Perhaps even more disconcertingly in the light of Paul's appeal to singleness in 1 Cor 7, 1 Timothy seemingly describes childbirth as a condition (or means?) for women's salvation, "provided they continue in faith and love and holiness, with modesty" (2:15)—although we have to hold this together with the author's concern regarding false teachers who have started forbidding marriage altogether (4:3).[49]

---

46. Hellerman, *When the Church Was a Family*, 91.

47. Towner, *Letters*, 360.

48. LaFosse, "Women, Children and House Churches," 390.

49. 1 Tim 2:15 is a notoriously difficult verse for the translators of the Bible; for an overview of some of the issues of its interpretation, see Hutson, "'Saved through Childbearing.'"

How are we to understand this noticeable tension between two different visions for the Christian life? Life never stands still. New situations require a fresh response, and that was certainly true of the second and third generation of Christians making sense of their faith and life together. By this time, the eyewitnesses of Jesus had passed away. Volatility and harassment by the imperial authorities often marked the life of Christian communities. But the Christian movement continued to grow; a lot of believers were now living in and as Christian households, negotiating their lives in the all-pervading climate of Roman household structure and legal pressure to marry. Shedding some of the loose "enthusiastic" organization in which the language of siblingship predominated, these communities were now adopting a more hierarchical, orderly structure which was much more in line with that of the traditional Roman household.[50]

The household codes within the New Testament may also be an attempt to emphasize that, despite the accusations, Christians were not the enemy of society.[51] Thus, for instance, 1 Timothy expresses a determination to give "the adversary no occasion to revile us," and in the light of that instructs younger widows to marry and reproduce (1 Tim 5:14)—in other words, to take upon traditional responsibilities of women in Roman society. As we have seen earlier, women's place in family and society was hotly debated among the Romans, and some of this debate is reflected in the life of the New Testament churches.[52]

It is, of course, easy to judge this from the safe distance of our twenty-first century. Some see in these household codes the weakening of the "new family" ethos of brothers and sisters championed by Jesus.[53] Others consider it a justifiable compromise if Christianity was to survive in an "inevitably flawed and imperfect society. . . . If we can envisage first century Christianity having a choice between revolution and transformation from within, then we have to say that Christianity chose the second."[54]

Indeed, a careful look reveals that these household instructions subtly subvert some of the usual expectations of Roman family relationships. Spousal relationships are to reflect the love between Christ and the church (Eph 5:25–32). In contrast to other, non-Christian variants of household codes, not only the wives and children are addressed and instructed, but so are the husbands, masters, and parents. Even more unexpectedly for the culture of the

50. Horrell, "From ἀδελφοί," 310.

51. Dunn, "Household Rules," 54–55.

52. Osiek and Balch, *Families in the New Testament World*, 217.

53. Sanders, *Ethics*, 73–76, 79–80.

54. Dunn, "Household Rules," 61.

time, slaves are addressed directly (see, for instance, Eph 6:7), signaling that they are considered to be members of the community rather than "property."[55]

In some ways, these passages give us a glimpse into an early example of the task of interpreting and applying the message of Jesus which will have to be faced by each new Christian generation. Lisa Sowle Cahill puts it this way: "The household codes model a *process* of interpretation, wherein the family is constantly challenged and redefined by its Christian identity, even as it responds to other historical and cultural influences, in an ongoing dynamic of formation and transformation."[56]

However, the turn taken by this second- and third-generation Christianity can also serve as a cautionary tale. In adopting and adapting these household codes, the church chose to minimize the earlier predominant language and ethos of a family of brothers and sisters, which was so radically different from the father-centered families of the empire. Feminist theologians would be quick to point out that "this strategy for survival gradually introduced the patriarchal-societal ethos of the time into the church."[57] The language of brothers and sisters did not get completely lost, but it disappeared from the fore; this is a reality that is ours to wrestle with even today as we seek meaningful Christianity.

Timothy and His Widows

> Implicitly (although subject to ideological suspicion) a celibate option remained even for younger widows, if they were able to maintain themselves or found someone within or outside their family who was willing to support them.[58]

Further interesting issues arise if we read these texts more attentively, "between the lines," so to speak. The very fact that the author of 1 Tim 5:3–16 feels the need to encourage young widows to marry signals that there was a substantial group of those who were not in a rush to do so.[59] If these widows remained single and were without a male guardian, they would have had to be financially supported by the church. The passage questions the motivation of these women to remain widows, suggesting that they were "living for

---

55. Cahill, "Christian Social Perspective," 168.

56. Cahill, "Christian Social Perspective," 169. Emphasis in the original.

57. Schüssler Fiorenza, *In Memory of Her*, 266.

58. Seim, *Double Message*, 240.

59. MacDonald, "Reading 1 Corinthians," 40.

pleasure" (5:6) at the expense of the Christian community. Such a behavior (subsidized by the church!) would have also impacted the reputation of the Christian movement amongst the Roman traditionalists, already outraged at the new freedoms claimed by women in society.[60] Instead, the letter urges the church to concentrate on supporting the ones who are truly in need: those without children and legal as well as financial protection.

In 1 Timothy, we can also discern the beginnings of a "women's house" supported by a well-to-do believer who can provide for a community of widows in her care (1 Tim 5:16). Having such a supporter may have opened the door for younger widows to remain unmarried too.[61] In any case, it encouraged those within the church able to provide for other sisters in Christ, to do so and thus alleviate the financial burden that otherwise would be borne by the community. As we shall see in the next chapter, communities of unmarried, chaste Christians will continue growing in importance over the next decades and centuries, paving a way for a very particular understanding of the best way to live a Christian life.

---

60. Towner, *Letters to Timothy and Titus*, 335.

61. Seim, *Double Message*, 239–40.

4

Living Like Angels

Early Christianity

That Christians were suspected of political subversion and of threatening the societal order and institutions of the patriarchal house comes again and again to the fore in pagan attacks against Christianity in the second and third century.[1]

By the end of the second century, there could have been as many as five million people practicing some version of Christianity—from the perspective of the empire, an illegal and dangerous cult.[2] As those who refused to worship the emperor, they were at risk of being blamed—by the authorities, or the mob, or both—for whatever was going wrong in the empire. Maltreatment of Christians was often localized and sporadic, but the general view was that Christianity was an expression of atheism and the "hatred of the human race."[3] Romans perceived their disregard for the confines and the patterns of the traditional household as an opposition to the empire and its values: after all, in their meetings Christian men and women mixed together, and slaves were allowed into worship and addressed as "brothers" and "sisters." Some suspected that Christian meetings involved "drunken orgies [as well as] incest and some horrid rituals involving a tethered dog."[4]

1. Schüssler Fiorenza, *In Memory of Her*, 265.

2. Brown, *Body and Society*, 138.

3. Tacitus, *Ann.* 15.44.

4. Minucius Felix, *Octavius*, quoted in Frend, "Persecutions," 509. It would not be the last time that various Christian groups were accused of such things. Many centuries later, I grew up in the Soviet atheist regime, acutely aware of rumors about "those horrible Baptists who call themselves Christians" that were shared amongst my townsfolk. As Baptists,

Accusations of incest, no doubt, were kindled by the sibling language used amongst Christians as well as the practice of the holy kiss (e.g., 1 Thess 5:26). The kiss (which would have been a full kiss on the mouth) was traditionally shared between family members as well as lovers—a testament to the continuing self-identification of Christians as the new family of God's people.[5] In such a climate, Christian leaders often sought to underline that their Christian faith contained no indecency. Thus the *Letter to Diognetus* (probably written in the second century) seeks to demonstrate that as far as human relations go, Christians were, in fact, "like all others": "they marry, as do all [others]; they beget children, but they do not destroy their offspring. They have a common table, but not a common bed."[6]

Yet not all Christians opted for marriage and children. An apocryphal document titled *Acts of Paul and Thecla* recounts how Thecla, a girl from a prominent family, renounced her family and her fiancée upon hearing Paul preach. Her own mother and fiancée were so incensed that they brought Thecla to the governor to be burned alive. She was, however, miraculously delivered from martyrdom and later became a co-apostle with Paul.[7]

Thecla's story was very popular amongst early Christians. Its message was a significant and a formative one for the practice of celibacy and, through celibacy, for the vindication of the role of women as teachers of the faith. It also highlights the fury these women's actions stoked in a society which considered them a direct challenge to the duty of a woman to marry and bear children.[8]

What is also interesting is the "punch" in Paul's message according to the *Acts of Paul and Thecla*: "You will not be raised from the dead unless you remain chaste, abstain from polluting the flesh, and guard your chastity." The retort of Paul's opponents is equally telling: "This resurrection which [Paul] claims is about to happen has already occurred in the children we have had."[9] Once again we can note the tension between producing children as a central value of Roman society or Jewish people of God, and a radical renunciation of reproduction as a sign of the Christian kingdom to come. In an environment where many children had to be born so that at least some of them would survive into adulthood, a refusal to do one's duty in producing future members of society might have indeed looked like the "hatred of the human race." The fact that, as *Diognetus* would want to stress, Christians did not practice abortion

---

we were apparently "known" to practice sexual orgies and sacrifice newborn babies.

5. Meeks, "Social and Ecclesial Life," 170.

6. *Diognetus* 5.6.

7. "The Acts of Thecla," 41, in Ehrman, *Lost Scriptures*, 121.

8. Kraemer and D'Angelo, *Women and Christian Origins*, 250.

9. "The Acts of Thecla," 12, 14, in Ehrman, *Lost Scriptures*, 116.

or, in contrast to their pagan neighbors, abandon their newborns, was not enough to shift the anti-Christian sentiment. At least not for a while.

Sexual Asceticism under the Gnostic Influence

Celibacy is at Christianity's core, the story of a divine infant miraculously born to a human, virgin mother.[10]

As it kept expanding, the Christian movement wrestled with different perspectives on marriage and singleness. Much of what we know of the first few centuries comes either from writings later deemed to be heretical (or at least not quite trustworthy—many of them rediscovered only recently), or from their Christian opponents who were later recognized as representing the orthodox Christian position, and are commonly known as the "church fathers." (Yes, there is an irony here given what Jesus had to say about calling no one "father.") These writings reveal tensions which existed in the early churches between promoting celibacy and upholding marriage.

As we will see in a moment, the majority of Christians continued to marry or cohabit. However, the second and third centuries CE saw an incredible phenomenon: people who, like Thecla, refused to marry. Such refusals to marry soon acquired a very particular focus—namely, virginity, or at least, celibacy. Rather than being about freedom from the shackles of marital responsibilities, the notion of staying unmarried for Christ's sake became increasingly focused on keeping the body pure.

One of the major reasons for this development is the prominence of Neoplatonic philosophy which saw the sexual urges, the body, and indeed all the material world as opposing the soul's communion with the divine. Such an understanding of the world was extremely popular, especially due to a movement commonly known as Gnosticism (named thus for its placing particular emphasis on a special knowledge—*gnōsis* in Greek—required to obtain salvation). The lines between Gnosticism and what later became known as "orthodox" Christianity were rather blurred, and there was great diversity among different groups, gnostic or not, claiming to be Christian. The Neoplatonic devaluation of the physical world had a great influence on various Christian groups, and was frequently adopted, and adapted, by the growing number of theologians and philosophers who identified themselves as Christians.

There were several ways to think about the divide or enmity between the body and the soul. First of all, let us look at the extreme ends of the spectrum.

10. Abbott, *History*, 17.

One of them was to consider the physical world as of no importance for the soul, and therefore to condemn the practice of marriage as a thing of "this passing age," but to allow sexual relations within the community, as an extension of all things that were to be held in common. We see mentions of such groups (for example, a sect called Nicolaitans, possibly connected to the group mentioned in Rev 2:6 and 2:15), but we know them only through their opponents—that is, the writings of the church fathers in which they take a strong stance against such views.

At the other end of the spectrum—and much more widespread—was a teaching that marriage and sex were simply incompatible with the Christian way, and therefore were to be unreservedly renounced. Confirming the New Testament concerns about the false teachers who "forbid marriage and demand abstinence from foods" (1 Tim 4:3), these ascetics rejected not only marriage and marital sex, but also meat and wine—on the basis that these, too, would not have been consumed before the fall and the expulsion from paradise.[11] Commonly known as Encratites, these groups saw sexuality itself as "the way of the animals" that the serpent had taught Eve.[12] For them, the escape from the curse of the present age, and to the paradise of heaven, was through "the boycott of the womb," which sometimes went alongside taking in abandoned children.[13]

Such views were especially prominent in early Syrian Christianity, to the degree that celibacy was considered to be a requirement for baptism.[14] Those who were already married were admonished to cease their sexual relations. In one of the texts which originated from among the Syrian churches, an apocryphal piece of work called *The Acts of Thomas*, Jesus appears to a newly married couple in the bridal chamber and persuades them to "refrain from this filthy intercourse," to be free from the burden of raising children, and instead to trust that they will be blessed with spiritual children. The couple are convinced, and join "in a different marriage," of a spiritual kind.[15]

In order to understand this growing focus on virginity and chastity, we need to appreciate that the very act of withdrawing from what was assumed to be an essential aspect of human life was a proclamation of the beginning of the end for "this world," and the beginning of the eternal life. To control or deny the urges for sleep, food, and sex, typically associated with the mortality of the body, meant to experience some of that future transformation already in the

---

11. Shaw, "Sex and Sexual Renunciation," 365.

12. Brown, *Body and Society*, 95.

13. Brown, *Body and Society*, 99, 101.

14. Voobus, *Celibacy*.

15. "The Acts of Thomas," 12, 14, in Ehrman, *Lost Scriptures*, 126–27.

present, and to prefigure what was to come. To renounce sex in particular was "to throw a switch located in the human person; and, by throwing that precise switch, it was believed possible to cut the current that sustained the sinister *perpetuum mobile* of life in 'the present age.'"[16] As far as many ascetics were concerned, this was what it meant to be "like angels."

Importantly, however, it was not so much the bodily condition that defined one's virginity, but intent. It was something one could "become," and as such, it was available not only to those who were physically virgins, but also to the married or widowed. They, too, could become virgins.[17] One of the church fathers, Tertullian, advised a widower to take "a spiritual wife"—that is, to marry, but abstain from sexual relationship—if he really could not get by without someone to manage the household, spin the wool, and prepare the food.[18] Such an arrangement would have been particularly convenient for Christian men by allowing them to remain "untainted" by sex, but have the practicalities of domestic life taken care of.

What we see, then, is a particular focus on abstaining from sexual relationships as the shortest route to the heavenly life. Or as another church father, Cyprian, wrote to the celibates: "That which we shall be, you have already begun to be. . . . You already possess the glory of the resurrection. . . . You pass through the world without contagion, like the angels of God."[19] Remarkably, this path was now available to all Christians—including women. Any of them, writes historian Peter Brown, "could achieve reputations for sexual abstinence as stunning as those achieved by any cultivated male."[20] In the next section, we will look at their experience in those early years of Christianity.

Early Christian Women Celibates

It was left to Christian treatises on virginity to speak in public on the physical state of the married woman—on their danger in childbirth, on the pain in their breasts during suckling, on their exposure to children's infections, on the terrible shame of

16. Brown, *Body and Society*, 85.

17. McNamara, *New Song*, 108–9.

18. Tertullian, *Exh. cast.* 12.2.

19. Cyprian, *Hab. virg.* 22–23, in Osiek and Balch, *Families in the New Testament World*, 152.

20. Brown, *Body and Society*, 61.

infertility, and on the humiliation of being replaced by servants in their husbands' affections.[21]

We do not know the actual numbers, but by the second century numerous women were embracing virginity. The same period was marked by the growing interest in the life and role of Mary, the mother of Jesus, especially in places where stories of her birth, childhood, and adolescence started to circulate in the form of a second-century text called the Protevangelium of James. The story of Mary's perpetual virginity became a symbol of purity and an inspiration for those seeking pious life.

Eschatological motivation apart, other factors also made virginity particularly attractive as a viable alternative to marriage from a woman's perspective. Freedom from marriage and sexual intercourse presented an opportunity for a woman to exercise much greater control over her own affairs, her own time, and her environment. It also meant control over her own body and freedom from such risks of marital life as pregnancy and childbirth. Many other women who did marry had a possibility of finding such freedom later in life through embracing widowhood. As one's husband was typically considerably older, many women outlived their husbands and then faced a choice between remarriage or widowhood. For a number of them, widowhood became the desired route.

We have already noted that widows had constituted a significant group in the New Testament churches, and a hint to an "order" of widows supported by the church can be found in 1 Tim 5:9–11. Many Christian women continued the tradition, taking the vow of chastity and embracing the duties of a Christian widow: visiting and nursing the sick, supporting the poor, instructing younger women, and, especially in the Eastern churches, serving as deaconesses. Such a choice was viewed overwhelmingly positively by the rest of the church. Tertullian addressed the widows considering remarriage with this passionate question: "Why do you reject the freedom that is given to you in returning to the bonds of matrimony?"[22]

Of course, the answer to this rhetorical question depended on the widow's social status. Many of them would have been very poor, and not remarrying would have meant a risk of extreme poverty. However, the increasing respect for the status of a widow and the support system organized by the church meant that "a life as a widow was not only desirable; it was also rendered feasible."[23] Indeed, the well-to-do widows often played an important role in

---

21. Brown, *Body and Society*, 25.

22. Tertullian, *Ux.* 1.8, quoted in Nathan, *Family*, 45.

23. Seim, *Double Message*, 235.

enabling the work of the theologians and entire churches. A fourth-century theologian, Jerome, is a particularly good example of a church leader who discussed the role of widows at great length while being funded by two ascetic widows, Marcella and Paula. The two women featured prominently in his correspondence and funded his projects, including the translation of the Bible into Latin.

For women, both virginity and widowhood enabled something nigh impossible: namely, transcending the confines of gender and sexual difference. In the Roman world, they were regarded as "failed men," passive, and ruled by their bodies and emotions. The very act of claiming power over one's body meant that these women were seen, and saw themselves, as more than women, or even no longer women—so much so that they were at times actually described as having "become male."[24] Some cut their hair; some left their husbands; and some adopted male clothing as a way of claiming equality in Christian ministry, in choirs, in teaching and assisting in baptizing other women, or the distribution of communion to women at home. Older celibate women, especially widows with property, were able to transform their own home into a celibate community of prayer, fasting, and sacred study.

However, the independence of such women did make the (male) church leadership increasingly uncomfortable. Not only were these women traveling and organizing their lives as they saw best fit for the purposes of serving the kingdom of God, but they were also challenging the accepted notions of what it meant to be a woman. Moreover, some virgins, while being committed to chastity, wore beautiful clothing and jewelry and attended baths and parties, creating yet another challenge to the perception of celibate womanhood.[25] Not surprisingly, a number of church fathers had a few things to say on the subject. In his tract named *On the Veiling of Virgins*, Tertullian states that the virgins could not claim any of the privileges not available to married women of the time, "such as speaking in church, teaching, baptizing, or holding ecclesiastical offices."[26] At the Synod of Elvira, in early fourth century, it was decided that both virgins and widows were required to "take public vows and wear prescribed, identifiable clothing."[27] In these rulings, we can recognize a much more regulated form of celibacy which would eventually enclose the Christian virgin in the walls of a monastery.

---

24. Osiek and Balch, *Families in the New Testament World*, 153.

25. McNamara, *New Song*, 116–17.

26. Salisbury, *Church Fathers*, 123.

27. Salisbury, *Church Fathers*, 6.

Early Christians and Marriage

> How beautiful, then, the marriage of two Christians. . . . Side by side, they visit God's church and partake of God's banquet; side by side, they face difficulties and persecution, share their consolations. They have no secrets from one another and never shun each other's company; they never bring sorrow to each other's hearts. . . . They need not be furtive about making the Sign of the Cross, nor timorous in greeting the brethren, nor silent in asking the blessing of God. . . . Hearing and seeing this, Christ rejoices. To such as these he gives his peace. Where there are two together, there also he is present; and where he is, evil is not.[28]

Not everybody subscribed to the Encratite teaching. Virginity and celibacy may have been extolled, but the majority of Christians did marry and have children—although in contrast to the imperial culture, Christian marriage was meant to be for a lifetime. One of the most passionate descriptions of Christian marriage is by Tertullian in the quote above, where he imagines the support that Christian spouses can provide to each other in the midst of persecution and hardships. Similarly, Clement of Alexandria—himself a married man—saw chastity as God's gift, rather than something that humans could achieve by their own powers, or something that should be imposed upon others. There was nothing shameful, Clement argued, about being a married Christian: marriage was "co-operation with the work of creation."[29]

However, in comparison to how marriage was described in various passages of the New Testament, significant changes appear in the church fathers' vision for married life. As we have seen earlier, while the culture-at-large, both Greco-Roman and Jewish, saw marriage as the vehicle for producing children, the New Testament is conspicuously silent about having children being the "point" of it all. A few early theologians voiced a similar understanding. Tertullian, for example, noted that while pagans married for such reasons as "anxiety for posterity, and the bitter, bitter pleasure of children," to Christians who married, "this is idle."[30] Yet his was a minority view among the fathers, whose understanding of marriage became remarkably aligned to those of the empire in this respect. Justin Martyr summed it up this way: if "we marry, it is only that we may bring up children."[31] Frequent intercourse was not encouraged

---

28. Tertullian, *Ux.* 2, quoted in McNamara, *New Song*, 94–95.

29. Clement of Alexandria, *Strom.* 3.66, in Oulton and Chadwick, *Alexandrian Christianity*, 71.

30. Tertullian, *Ux.* 1.5.

31. Justin, *1 Apol.* 1.29.

either: quality was to trump quantity, and quality in this case meant producing children.[32] It followed from there that if a marriage had already produced children, then remarriage after the death of one's spouse was unnecessary.[33]

Many church fathers were also perturbed by "mixed marriages"—that is, Christian women marrying pagans. (The very fact that they had to argue this point with a great passion indicates that such marriages were common.) Tertullian's adversary, Callistus, Bishop of Rome—himself a former slave—went even further in this direction, issuing a decree allowing Christian women of high social status to live in "just concubinage" with lower-class or even enslaved men whom they could not legally marry—as long as they were both Christians and it was to be a permanent relationship. This created a considerable upset amongst his contemporaries, but the very fact that Callistus resorted to such a measure is telling: there seemed to be a significant shortage of potential husbands for Christian women. Indeed, this may indicate that early Christianity was particularly attractive to women, perhaps because of the Christian opposition to the pagan practices of abortion and infanticide.[34]

Yet in some ways, arguments about the propriety (or otherwise) of just concubinage were secondary questions. After all, as soon as one was engaged in sexual activity and shackled oneself to a coupled life, one was already a second-class Christian, compared to the higher ways of virgins and celibates. What emerged in those early Christian centuries was a "hierarchy of holiness" in which marriage represented the lowest category, below widowhood and virginity.[35] The words of another church father, Eusebius, describe this hierarchy of holiness best:

> Two ways of life were given by the law of Christ to his church. The one is above nature, and beyond common human living; it admits not marriage, childbearing, property, the possessing of wealth, but wholly and permanently separate from the common customary life of humanity, it devotes itself to the service of God alone in its wealth of heavenly love. And the other, more humble, more human, permits people to join in pure nuptials and to produce children, to undertake government, to give orders to soldiers fighting for right; it allows them to have minds for farming, for trade, and the other more secular interests as well as for religion; and it is for

32. Brown, *Body and Society*, 18.

33. Osiek and Balch, *Families in the New Testament World*, 148.

34. Stark, *Rise of Christianity*, 95–128, 240.

35. Cyprian (3rd cent.) compares these to the thirty, sixty, and hundredfold harvest of Mark 4:20. Osiek and Balch, *Families in the New Testament World*, 153. Tertullian, *Exh. to cast.* 1; Cyprian, *Hab. virg.* 21.

them that times of retreat and instruction and days for hearing sacred things are set apart. And a kind of secondary grade of piety is attributed to them.[36]

This kind of a "secondary grade of piety" would dominate the attitude towards Christian marriage for the next millennium and more, as the number of those calling themselves Christians continued to increase, and as the pagan world of the Roman Empire gave way for the new world of Christendom.

36. Eusebius, *Dem. ev.* 1.8, quoted in Allison, *Resurrecting Jesus*, 29.

5

After Constantine

Singleness and Marriage in Christendom

Christendom and the Rise of Monasticism

> The emperor Constantine Augustus to the people: Those who used
> to be classified as unmarried in the law of the old are to be freed
> from the menacing terrors of the law and are to live as if numbered
> among the married and supported by the bond of marriage, and
> all shall enjoy the equal legal status of taking such inheritances as
> each is entitled to. Nor indeed is anyone to be classified as child-
> less: the specified financial losses for this category shall not harm
> them. We deem that this measure shall also apply to women.[1]

The above quote from Emperor Constantine's revocation of the sanc-
tions against the unmarried and the childless reflects one aspect of the
profound change sweeping through the Roman Empire in the early fourth
century. As a recognition of the Christian devotion to the ideal of virginity,
it was signaling a momentous shift—though not a sudden one—which saw
Christianity emerge as the empire's official religion and a political institution.
Constantine decided to side with this previously persecuted, yet ever increasing movement—and more specifically, with a particular branch of this movement. As a result, not only was Constantine's political power consolidated, but
also was that of particular church leaders, who shortly became imperial bishops. Very soon, Constantine would be convening church councils, centraliz-

---

1. *Theodosian Code* 8.16.1, in Lee, *Pagans and Christians*, 200.

ing church government, and consolidating a unified body of Christian beliefs as well as practice. A new kind of union—that of church and the empire—was consummated, to be protected and sustained over the following centuries by the emperors of an increasingly divided East and West of the imperial world. As we explore how singleness and marriage were viewed and lived out across Christendom over the next millennium, we will focus particularly on the developments in the West, although at times for specific purposes we will also be visiting the Eastern part of the empire.

As the status of Christianity changed from persecuted to tolerated to preferred, and finally to the only legitimate religion, many changes also occurred within the church. One of these key changes was the surge of people seeking to become monks and nuns. In the last chapter, we saw how virginity had already become the most esteemed way of life among the persecuted Christians of the empire. Now, Christianity's political advance ushered in a new age for those seeking salvation through a radical renunciation of their bodies. For one thing, with penalties for the unmarried and childless abolished, the desire to forgo marriage was no longer hindered by law. For another, many of these Christians were increasingly disenchanted with the rapidly changing face of the church, now wedded to power, prestige, and a dilution of previously held ways of living and believing. Countless Christians flocked to uninhabited places, whether to live on their own or in a group of fellow monastics, seeking to recreate that original "singleness of heart" which they felt now was missing in the church.[2]

Some of them, like John of Egypt, chose complete seclusion—in John's case, carving his abode out of rock on the top of a cliff, or in one of the most dramatic instances, Symeon the Stylite making a pillar his home. Others became wanderers, beggars, prophets, or apostolic teachers, like Kashish, bishop of the island of Chios, who for thirteen years is said to have roamed the world in poor man's clothes. Still others joined monastic communities—sometimes as small as two or three monks, in other cases as large as several thousand—which again varied in their particular rhythms of life. Monasteries like Kellia in Egypt combined life in seclusion during the weekdays with monks coming together for weekend meals and communal liturgies. In different ways, throughout the empire, "monks and nuns made plain that, for some Christians at least, the kingdom had come: they had made for themselves a world without marriage and without private fields."[3]

This was a spiritual, but also a social alternative: a *different* kind of a family, a household unlike the households of the world. The vision of a new family

2. Brown, *Body and Society*, 226.
3. Brown, *Body and Society*, 435.

was especially clearly expressed in the monastery. It offered a new home for people who had already lost or were rejected by their biological kin, as well as for those who underwent a significant change in their circumstances, such as the death of a child, parents, or a spouse, an undesired betrothal, and even what we today refer to as the "empty nest syndrome."[4] And if relatives joined the same monastery, their relationship also altered, with efforts often made to separate them in their daily monastic living.[5]

Like worldly families, the spiritual family of God was to be fruitful, but its fruitfulness was to be of a different order. The imagery of a monk as a mother is particularly fascinating: carrying a powerful message of spiritual reproduction, it epitomized mothering up until the Victorian times, when the ideal of a woman as a biological mother came to the fore. Monks could speak of the nurture of novices as those "with whom I was in travail with much labor and to whom I have given birth."[6] Or, in the description of the life of Euthymios the Younger, one "labored to give birth to his disciple through the Bible, . . . wrapped him in the swaddling clothes of prayers and admonitions, and nourished him with the milk of virtue and the life-giving bread of divine knowledge."[7]

For many women of early Christendom, monasticism started at home. Such was the case of Macrina the Younger, a wealthy young woman who, after the death of her fiancé, decided to stay unmarried. Continuing to live in her parental home, she adopted a simple daily rhythm of prayer and work, and gradually turned her home into a religious community. Countless other women followed Macrina's path. One Egyptian report claims: "In every house of Christians, it is needful that there be a virgin, for the salvation of the whole house is that one virgin"—a reflection of the increasingly closer link being made between sexual purity and access to God, its power not limited to the virgins themselves, but extending to their families.[8]

---

4. Talbot, "Byzantine Family," 121.

5. Krawiec, *Shenoute*, 169.

6. Makarios Choumnos, quoted in Talbot, "Byzantine Family," 121.

7. Talbot, "Byzantine Family," 121.

8. *Canons of Athanasius* 98, quoted in Brown, *Body and Society*, 264. While at times choosing celibacy clearly was the choice of the young girl herself, at other times it was influenced by her family's interest in being relieved of dowry payments and other costs associated with raising a female. Offering her as a gift to the church was an attractive option. One of the church fathers, Basil of Caesarea, complained: "Parents, brothers and other relatives bring forward many girls before the proper age, not because the girls have an inner urge towards continence, but in order that their relatives may gain some material advantage from so doing." Brown, *Body and Society*, 261.

Church fathers were supportive of female monasticism, and were often keen to depict it as an alternative to various possible tragedies of family life. The list of these potential disasters was long indeed: the shame of not being able to produce children; the risk involved in pregnancy and childbirth; the fear for the children's lives as they grew; the possibility of the husband's infidelity or violence; responsibilities of managing the household; and so on. Gregory of Nyssa was convinced that "if only, before experience comes, the results of experience could be learnt . . . then what a crowd of deserters would run from marriage into the virgin life."[9]

As noted earlier, female virgins could transcend some of the confines of their gender—from enjoying the luxury of solitude of the cell to relationships far beyond the confines of a typical family circle. Such an opportunity would be especially apparent in the case of abbesses and wealthy foundresses, exercising their leadership within and beyond their monastic community. Abbess Hilda, for example, who founded a double monastery at Whitby under her own leadership, was said by Bede, a fellow monk, theologian, and historian, to have such a great wisdom "that not only ordinary people but even kings and princes asked and received her advice when they needed it."[10] Hildegard of Bingen—a highly learned and gifted noblewoman turned nun—became a renowned spiritual counselor whose consultations were sought by the pope and the emperors.

The Monastic Body

> What is this mystery in me? What is the principle of this mixture of body and soul? How can I be my own friend and my own enemy? Speak to me, my yoke-fellow, my nature![11]

While female virgins were acquiring responsibilities and roles not available to ordinary women, the male monks' relationship to Christ was often wrapped in the feminine language and sensual imagery of being Christ's lovers, spouses, and brides. The writings of the monks often display an awareness of the complex connection between body and soul, the bodily urges telling the story of the inner life, still awaiting their transformation, as illustrated by the cry of a Byzantine monk, John Climacus, quoted above.

---

9. Gregory of Nyssa, *Virg.* 28.1, quoted in Harrison, "Silent Majority," 93.

10. Ward, *Bede's Ecclesiastical History*, 132–33.

11. John Climacus, quoted in Egan, *Anthology*, 117.

Different answers to this cry in the monastic experience reflect the whole scale of responses to human sexuality: from negation and mortification of the body, to wrestling with temptation, to slipping up and committing sexual transgression, whether in fantasy, with a fellow monastic, or a member of the opposite sex, to insights into sublimating and rediscovering sexual desire through creative outlets and mystical experiences. Regarding the latter, St. Symeon the Theologian describes his own encountering of the divine in these erotically charged words:

> He himself is discovered within myself
> resplendent in the interior of my miserable heart,
> illuminating me on all sides with His immortal splendor,
> lighting up all my members with brightness,
> entirely intertwined with me, He embraces me totally. . . .
> I share in the light, I participate in the glory,
> and my face shines like my Beloved's,
> and all my members become bearers of light.[12]

However, instructions on the monastic life generally reveal a deep mistrust of the human ability to deal with desire. The right and proper environment was needed to keep the monks and nuns pure, which resulted in the increasing institutionalization of monasticism. Granted, there were some exceptions. In the British Isles, for example, an idea that caught the imagination of a number of devout men was that of *peregrination*—becoming a stranger to one's own place and country in order to wander for the love of God, perhaps to the far-off heathen lands. Such holy wandering often arose out of these men's unease with the unholy compromises that were being struck between the monasteries, churches, and secular powers. But overall, the monastery became the most common form of the monastic life. The *Benedictine Rule*, written by Benedict of Nursia in the sixth century, became the standard model of monastic life in the West. Requiring the monk to commit to a lifetime in a particular monastery and obedience to its abbot, the Rule offered a rhythm of manual labor and prayer. Similarly, in the Eastern part of the empire it was John Climacus in the early seventh century whose *Ladder of Divine Ascent* became the normative text for Eastern monasticism. For John, holy wandering was a temptation that a monk must resist. Instead, one was to seek the constant presence of God—the angelic state—by the transformation of the body: "To have mastered one's body is to have taken command of nature, which is

---

12. *Hymns* 16.23–23, quoted in Krueger, "Homoerotic Spectacle," 112.

surely to have risen above it. And the man who has done this is not much lower than the angels, if even that."[13]

Over the following centuries, monasticism continued to evolve, as did its relationship to the rest of the church and the powers that be. Some monasteries and orders became centers of enormous wealth and power, while others struggled to survive. New orders kept springing up at different times, some out of a desire to renew the monastic call to the simple life or learning, and others in the name of the holy war against the pagans which they wanted to wage as warrior monks, acquiring vast territories in the process. As ever, wealth and power frequently gave rise to stories of laxity and various abuses. The notorious corruption of some of the monks and nuns, including their sexual liaisons, eventually became one of the key catalysts of the Reformation, which we will explore in the next chapter. The same, indeed, can be said about another category of people who were increasingly required to abstain from marriage: the clergy. Let us look briefly at this development.

Priestly Celibacy

The example of the priests of the Old Testament who abstained from their wives when offering sacrifices was cited to claim that Christian priests, who continually offered sacrifice at the altar, must be in a permanent state of ritual purity, free from contact with women's polluting bodies.[14]

While most of the New Testament instructions regarding ordained church leadership assumed that they would be married, in Christendom's Western lands priests and deacons were increasingly expected to remain celibate. The theological point of celibacy also changed, as illustrated in the quote above: rather than being a sign of the in-breaking of the kingdom of God, and something that could be expressed by any Christian, male or female, it was now about "cultic purity" following the Levitical laws—"a Christian temple priesthood."[15] Of course, from the point of view of the institution that the church had become, spouseless and heirless priests were particularly convenient for the protection and expansion of church property.

Yet the actual process of enforcing priestly celibacy was long and complicated. Priests could easily be found openly living with a wife or concubine until clerical celibacy was emphatically enforced by the church councils in

13. Climacus, *Ladder*, 181.

14. Ruether, *Christianity and the Making of the Modern Family*, 49.

15. Ruether, *Christianity and the Making of the Modern Family*, 49.

the twelfth century. After then, many such relationships moved underground. But the move of the councils communicated the direction being taken by the Roman Catholic Church as it sought to gain more freedom from the secular powers of the time and to convey a clear theological message: ordained ministry required celibacy because sexual relations tainted one's suitability for holy service.

The church in the Eastern part of the empire, on the other hand, adopted a different pattern, which expected those ordinands who were already married to continue in marriage. Eventually all parish priests were expected to marry even before they were considered for ordination; celibacy was only required of bishops. This difference was a reflection of the deepening divide between the Eastern and Western churches.

Beyond Vowed Celibacy: Christendom's Other Singles

Maidens and wenches, remember the lesson you're about to hear.
Don't hurtle yourself into marriage far too soon. . . .
Though wedlock I do not decry:
Unyoked is best! Happy the woman without a man.[16]

While the monastery and, if you were living in the West, priesthood were the most obvious and permanent pathways of unmarried life, a significant proportion of lay people in Christendom were leading single lives too: servants, weavers, spinsters, prostitutes, guild members, and other city dwellers engaged in a trade or service which either prohibited or was complicated by married life.[17] Most unusually, even some peasant women—not the most likely category of singles—remained unmarried. Joan of Arc is, no doubt, best known among these, but an equally interesting, and different, story is that of a fourteenth-century English peasant, Cecilia Panifader of Brigstock, who made a decision to remain unmarried and ran her own household.

At this point, we will need to pause at one of the most interesting times of medieval Europe: the twelfth and thirteenth centuries, marked by a wave of religious revivals among lay people. Some of the expressions of this revival were eventually absorbed by the church, while others were vehemently opposed and suppressed. An example of the latter was the movement of the Cathars, also called Albigensians, who preached complete sexual abstinence

16. Poem by Anna Bijns, 1493–1575. Aercke, "Anna Bijns," 382.

17. The numbers vary from at least 10 percent to nearly half of the adult population, depending on the specific period and location. See, e.g., Kowaleski, "Singlewomen."

and the corruption of all that was physical. Because they denounced the Roman Catholic Church, they were fiercely persecuted, even earning their own crusade.

Cathars were an extreme case, but there were countless other wandering preachers, recluses, and hermits calling all people to an apostolic life of poverty and simplicity as the true essence of what Jesus had preached. Innumerable lay sisterhoods and brotherhoods sprang up. One of the most remarkable of such associations in Northern Europe was the Beguines—lay women who chose to embrace chastity and live together in communities called beguinages, or small "women's towns." Their buildings in places like Bruges, Leuven, and Amsterdam still stand as witnesses of the fascinating medieval worlds of these single women.

The Beguines typically engaged in the textile industry, teaching, or nursing. They formed closely knit communities, but they were not bound by permanent vows and were free to leave and marry at any point, taking with them all their movable property. Theirs was an organic movement: there was no center or leadership, and no particular Rule they all followed. Unsurprisingly, their life baffled their contemporaries: as one Franciscan friar put it, "we have no idea what to call [them], ordinary women or nuns, because they live neither in the world nor out of it."[18]

There were similar, though less prominent, associations of laymen too, most commonly known as Beghards. Belgian towns of the late thirteenth century were known for Beghard weavers who pooled their resources, sharing devotional life as well as taking care of those of the community who had grown old or ill; or in the case of some other Beghard groups, wandering and preaching against the abuse in the church.[19]

Historians continue to argue over the dominant motivation of such movements: were their reasons primarily socio-economic or religious? In some ways, the appearance of female communities in particular made perfect sense given that crusades and wars had cut down the number of potential husbands, which was further reduced by the celibacy of the priests and monks. Convents were often oversubscribed and so not always an option, especially for those who were poor. Banding with other women made it possible to strengthen one's economic security and wellbeing, and, in the words of historian Katherine Lynch, to become part of "one of the most interesting and 'original' examples of lay efforts to construct artificial families and communities within an urban setting."[20]

18. Gilbert of Tournai, quoted in Stoner, "Sisters Between," 1.

19. McDonnell, *Beguines and Beghards*, 275.

20. Lynch, *Individuals*, 80.

However, life in these communities also had a clear spiritual emphasis. Many Beguines were touched by monastic mysticism, and would live out their devotion "at mass and the daily hours, in devotional exercises, in song and dance, and in writing."[21] Here is a snippet from the striking wording of Mechthild of Magdeburg, a thirteenth-century German Beguine:

> The pull of God with which God drew the soul in the beginning to himself, has such great power that it awakens the soul so that she can taste God's sweetness.
>
> After that, it drives out all evil from the five senses.[22]

Beside the Beguines, other alternative spiritual families of single women sprang up elsewhere, such as the *beatas* or *filles seculières* in southern Europe.[23] The life of many of these associations was cut short by church authorities who did not like the freedom such communities were able to exercise, but some beguinages in the Low Countries continued, even up to recent times: the last Beguine in the world died in 2013.[24]

Stories of same-sex communities also raise a question about the life of same-sex attracted people. Unfortunately, historical evidence is scarce, save for a regular condemnation and penalties for homosexual acts as "going against nature," although their severity varied across the empire and at different times.[25] Unsurprisingly, homosexuality was a continuous concern for the senior clergy and monastic leaders, who guarded their monasteries and convents against "particular friendships." (On the other hand, there were some notable exceptions, such as Saint Aelred of Rievaulx's work on *Spiritual Friendship*, a work of great wisdom and insight about the gift of friendship.)

The roots of the harsh stance against homosexual relations lie in the prohibitions and condemnations of such behavior in Leviticus 18, which were quite likely set in contrast to the male transvestite priests serving in some Near East cults.[26] The death penalty for male homosexual acts was incorporated into Roman law when the empire was Christianized, and the condemnation of homosexuality was fixed in the official teaching of the Catholic Church in the thirteenth century through the work of Thomas Aquinas, one of its most influential theologians. Basing his thought on the philosophy of Aristotle and

21. Simons, "On the Margins," 322; see also McDonnell, *Beguines and Beghards*, 84–85.

22. Quoted in Poor, "Transmission and Impact," 101.

23. See Lynch, *Individuals, Families, and Communities*, 161–63. There were similar movements of men; see Lynch, *Individuals, Families, and Communities*, 89–102.

24. "Marcella Pattyn"; Abbott, *History*, 119.

25. Wiesner-Hanks, *Christianity and Sexuality*, 49.

26. Crompton, *Homosexuality and Civilization*, 39–43.

seeking to harmonize Christian teaching with natural law, Aquinas produced two reasons why homosexuality was against nature. First, even animals (he argued) did not engage in such behavior, and, second, as the purpose of sex was procreation, homosexual acts were going against this purpose and thus were sinful, alongside masturbation, "wrong" positions of heterosexual sex, and bestiality. In this respect, Aquinas argued, they were worse than rape and adultery, as the latter two at least may result in pregnancy.[27]

The concern, however, was particularly focused on male homosexuals; most of the time neither the church nor the secular rulers thought much about sexual relations between women. As one historian sums it up, "because in their minds sex always involved penetration, they had difficulty imagining sex without a penis."[28] Thus, two women boarding together or sharing an otherwise close relationship did not necessarily attract attention, provided that the relationship was discreet.[29]

Much more could be said about the experience of singleness by non-heterosexual people—but that would be a different book.[30] We must leave their story here, noting that in the climate of suspicions, penalties, and persecutions, many homosexuals either chose religious service or married members of the opposite sex. Some found long-term same-sex partners and lived in secrecy, and some of these found ways of celebrating a spiritual union that had clear parallels or even explicit references to marriage.[31] And so we turn next, then, to the experience and Christianization of heterosexual marriage.

Spiritual Marriages

> If virginity was an anticipation of the future kingdom, marriage was hopelessly bound to the temporal order—a constant reminder of our fallen state.[32]

Married people may have constituted the majority of the population, but they were aware that their position was at the bottom of the spiritual ranking scale. Here again we should note a particular view towards sex, the roots of which were much more in Gnosticism or Stoicism than in the teaching of Jesus and

27. Aquinas, *ST* II–II, q. 153. art. 2.

28. Wiesner-Hanks, *Christianity and Sexuality*, 37.

29. See, e.g., Hunt, "Sapphic Strain."

30. See, for instance, Crompton, *Homosexuality and Civilization*.

31. Boswell, *Same-Sex Unions*.

32. Elliott, *Spiritual Marriage*, 39.

Christian life we find in the pages of the New Testament. The writings of Ambrose, a fourth-century Bishop of Milan, sum up well the attitude that was to characterize Christendom up until the Reformation. His treatise, *Concerning Virginity*, stressed the perpetual chastity of the mother of Jesus, wife of Joseph: she was not touched by the "sin" of intercourse and "was a virgin not only in body but also in mind."[33]

Inspired by this model of Mary and Joseph (rather than, say, Paul's urge for the spouses to fulfil "conjugal debt" as expressed in 1 Cor 7:1–5), some couples sought to practice a celibate, or "spiritual," marriage. Some would vow virginity on their wedding night, whereas others would transition to chastity later on in life, after producing children. One of the best known of such couples was Melania the Younger and Pinian, a rich Roman family living at the turn of the fourth and the fifth centuries. Melania was attracted to celibacy from an early age, and it was further stirred by the trauma of the deaths of her two children, and almost dying herself at the second childbirth. Melania convinced Pinian to embrace celibacy and give away their vast joint fortunes. The couple founded numerous monasteries in different parts of the empire as they settled in North Africa, and later in Jerusalem, with Melania playing the leading role, continuing the projects after Pinian's death.

In later centuries, the church's attitude toward celibate marriages varied. At times, they were considered the preferred route for the priests who were already married, although "too many of these clerical couples lapsed into marital relations"[34] and so clearly this was not a lasting solution. At other times, chaste marriages were opposed, on the basis that it was nearly impossible to maintain an absolutely chaste relationship between the sexes, and also because spiritual marriage seemed to grant too much freedom to the wives, thus disrupting the accepted gender norms. At other times spiritual marriages received the "cool toleration" of the church.[35]

However, the implicit values of chaste marriage were clearly imprinted on the expectations for "regular" marriages. Sexual activity was to be restricted to producing children and limited to particular circumstances and times of the year—not on Sundays, Fridays, key saints' days, or during Lent, Advent, menstruation, pregnancy, or while nursing of a child. "This left about fifty days a year when a married couple could legitimately have sexual intercourse, and even this was hemmed in by restrictions as to position (prone, man on top), time of day (night only), and proper dress (at least partially clothed)."[36]

33. Ambrose, *Virg.* 2:2:7.
34. Elliott, "Chastity and Chaste Marriage," 124.
35. Elliott, *Spiritual Marriage*, 17.
36. Wiesner-Hanks, *Christianity and Sexuality*, 35.

Although it was a necessary activity for producing the next generation, sex—even within marriage—was directly linked to sin.

Augustine and the Goods of Marriage

> Abstention from all intercourse is better even than marital intercourse that takes place for the sake of procreation.[37]

It is now time to meet Augustine—a fourth/fifth-century North African theologian and one of the primary shapers of Western Christianity's theology. Whether or not we are conscious of it, his life, his ideas, and their consequences, still loom large today in our cultural heritage and in our own views, as well as our hang-ups, about sexuality. Looking at these in detail would take a whole chapter, or indeed a whole book: we would need to talk of Augustine's time as a follower of a dualist religion of the Manicheans, with its separation of the physical and the spiritual into the kingdoms of darkness and of light; his relationship with his concubine and the mother of his child, whom he was unable to marry and instead felt he had to send away; and his struggle with his own sexual energy, which led him to pray for God to give him chastity, "but not yet."[38]

We cannot do that here, and so instead will take a brief look at his main ideas on marriage and sexuality. Augustine felt compelled to follow the call of "Lady Continence"—which, like his contemporaries, he held to be the higher way than the married state. But, against some other theologians of the time, he also argued that marriage was a genuine "good," if still *inferior* to that of virginity and chastity. The three particular "goods of marriage" as Augustine saw them were procreation, fidelity, and sacrament. The emphasis on the first good, procreation, should not be surprising: it reflects the key element in a theology of marriage by most Christian theologians who wrote on the subject. However, quite significantly, for Augustine it was not the *only* good that defined marriage: whether it resulted in the birth of children or not, and whether there were sexual relations or not, marriage was still marriage.

One of the big debates of the time was whether sex and procreation were part of the original creation of God, or whether it was a consequence of sin. Augustine came to regard physical intercourse and the creation of family as part of the original creation, but without lust and therefore without sin. All of

37. Augustine, *Bon. conj.* 6.6.

38. Augustine, *Conf.* 8.7.17. For an excellent introduction to Augustine as a person and a thinker, see Brown, *Body and Society*, chapter 19.

that, he said, changed after the fall: desire became corrupted, resulting in each human infant being born into that corruption, or "original sin." For that reason, even in marriage, sex was marred by lust and shame, and not something that could ever be simply enjoyed, shame-free and guilt-free.

What, then, was to be at the center of the spouses' union, if not the marital bed? For Augustine, the key to marriage was the friendship of the spouses.[39] Here we can detect clear echoes of classical Rome's ideal of a married couple as a harmonious entity of shared purpose, but it also helps us understand Augustine's thought about the two other goods of marriage: fidelity and sacrament. Fidelity encompassed sexual exclusivity, but also the broader sense of loyalty in the relationship of the spouses, whatever changes may occur during their marriage. Sacrament signified the bond of marriage as sacred and therefore indissoluble until the death of the spouse—just like the church could not be separated from Christ.

Augustine's writings became the basis of the Western church's theology of marriage for the next millennium: the elevation of virginity and chastity over married life, yet also a recognition of the importance of the "goods" produced by marriage. Above all, the emphasis on the indissolubility of marriage came to shape the understanding of marriage amongst Christendom's people.

Medieval Marriages: Laws and Customs

> While Christian preachers and teachers had long envisioned Christian marriage in profound theological terms—indeed, as an image of Christ and the church—the reality often fell short of this ideal.[40]

The notion of indissolubility, in theory at least, put divorce out of the question, except for adultery. Even in the case of adultery, penance and reconciliation were recommended; and if a marriage ended in a separation or divorce, then one was to lead a celibate life until the death of one's spouse.

At least such was the official stance. What was actually happening on the ground amongst the Christianized peoples of Europe was much more complex. It is true that divorce as we understand it now was not possible, but abandonment, estrangement, or separation were far from unknown, as was taking up alternative sexual arrangements.[41] The period of the increasing

---

39. Augustine, *Bon. conj.* 9.9.

40. Hunter, *Marriage and Sexuality*, 34.

41. Nathan, *Family*, 48.

political collapse of the Roman Empire offers a good illustration. In the midst of these monumental changes, the church had to learn to relate to the various tribes and kingdoms which overran the Roman Empire and were gradually converting to Christianity. The chiefs of these people typically had a number of wives and concubines: this was their status symbol and the way of expanding and maintaining their influence; and for women involved, too, the arrangement was a possibility of increasing one's importance as well as wealth.[42] When Christianity became the adopted religion of these tribes, the powerful men continued to keep concubines, but increasingly started marrying once only, and securing heirs exclusively from marriage. As to the lower classes, their marriage patterns remained unregulated for much longer: their living arrangements and the legitimacy of their offspring were not considered important.

Thus, it took a long time for a particular shape and understanding of marriage to be enforced on Christendom's people. But by the twelfth century, the Catholic Church had developed its matrimonial law which regulated matters of marriage for all the subjects in the Western world. At the heart of the law was, as we have already seen with Augustine, the idea of Christian marriage as a sacrament—that is, a mysterious yet visible sign of God's grace, a symbol of Christ and church which therefore could not and should not be broken. A twelfth-century Church Council in Verona first declared marriage to be a sacrament, although at that time it was understood to be of a different order than Baptism, Eucharist, or Holy Orders. It would have to wait until the sixteenth century and the Council of Trent's decision to list marriage amongst the Catholic Church's seven sacraments and to prohibit informal or common-law marriages—that is, relationships based on mutual agreement and without any relation to the church (not that such arrangements disappeared after that).[43]

The result of these developments was a clear distinction between Christian marriage and any other sexual relationship, however long or short. A sexual liaison was not exactly a praiseworthy thing to do, but it was much less serious if it should be dissolved rather than to be trapped in an unhappy marriage—or having to find ways to prove that the marriage had never been valid. (Indeed, even until today, and especially in traditionally Catholic countries in Latin America or Eastern Europe, one could observe a reluctance to enter into

---

42. Ruether, *Christianity and the Making of the Modern Family*, 52.

43. Over the course of time most European countries adopted similarly strict legal definitions of what made a marriage valid. In some countries common-law marriages continued to be legally recognized; in England, for example, they continued until 1753 and in Scotland until 1940. Thane, *Happy Families?*, 18.

matrimony, with people choosing to cohabitate for years, or even enter a civil marriage, before marrying "in the church" and therefore for life.[44])

But what made a Christian marriage valid, or, conversely, invalid? Canon law was not quite clear. Some medieval theologians argued that consummation—the physical union of the couple—was the start and an essential condition for a marriage to be true. (It also represented one of the loopholes for having one's marriage annulled—if, that is, one could prove that marriage was never consummated.) This stance was not without theological problems, particularly in the light of the belief in the chaste yet true marriage of Mary and Joseph. In practice, too, numerous sexual liaisons were made without any intention of marrying, especially by those who had the means to get away with potential consequences.

Consequently, marriage came to be based on consent, particularly in the northwest of Europe, and as such played a significant role in an emergence of a distinctly different family structure.[45] In southeastern Europe people continued to live in extended families and married early, but in the late medieval northwestern European lands, a new pattern emerged amidst plague outbreaks, booming labor markets and increasing wages (particularly for women), and the growing classes of artisans and tradespeople. People started marrying much later, in their thirties and forties; indeed a significant proportion did not marry at all.[46] Consent as the norm meant families now had a significantly lesser role to play in the children's choice of a spouse. Establishing consent as the basis of marriage also led to the rise of couples eloping—that is, marrying secretly—which is why some theologians insisted that a marriage ceremony had to involve a priest or witnesses.[47]

The need to insist on a priest and ceremony illustrates the fact that in spite of the development of a sacramental theology of marriage, there had not been much by way of ritual to express its Christian nature: after all, this was an attempt of the church as an institution to "Christianize" marriage, a secular structure with its long and colorful history. Not until the late middle ages did the church blessing of a marriage became essential for the marriage to be valid; before then, people could have just as likely got married in a pub, in the house, or even in bed. All that mattered was that the couple consented to be married (and were able to prove it later, if required), and consequently were able to consummate their relationship.

---

44. Cf. Ruether, *Christianity and the Making of the Modern Family*, 244n67.

45. Hajnal, "European Marriage Patterns."

46. Coontz, *Marriage*, 127.

47. Wiesner-Hanks, *Christianity and Sexuality*, 37.

Indeed, the period between the expression of consent and the sexual intercourse—the betrothal—could be a prolonged one, particularly where the couple's families were involved and significant financial considerations were at stake. In principle, betrothal was not dissimilar to the Jewish tradition: we may recall Mary and Joseph's engagement and Joseph's intent to release or "divorce" her when she is found pregnant with a child he knows is not his. Betrothal allowed a stage in the relationship during which one could get to know the future spouse—at times including the sexual knowing—but from which one could potentially still withdraw. In many ways, before the betrothed couple actually started living together, "they were neither single nor married."[48]

With time, however, the length of the betrothal kept decreasing, and often became virtually inseparable from marriage, especially under the influence of the Reformation movements—a historical turn which overthrew the millennium-old hierarchy of holiness, and set marriage firmly at the center of a good and godly society. It is to this development that we turn our attention next.

---

48. Reynolds, *Marriage in the Western Church*, 315.

6

Towards the Romance of the Nuclear Family

From Reformations to Modernity

Reformation Time: Away with Celibacy, Marriage Is Better

> Although women are ashamed to acknowledge this, Scriptures and experience teach us that there is only one in several thousands to whom God gives the gift to live chastely in a state of virginity. . . . God so created [the woman's] body that she should be with a man and bear and raise children. The words of [Genesis 1] clearly state this, and the members of her body sufficiently show that God himself formed her for this purpose.[1]

The later Middle Ages was a dramatic time for Western Europe. Dissatisfaction with the church and widespread corruption within its walls and systems were rife. Meanwhile, Eastern Christianity's spiritual center, Constantinople, had fallen, and large parts of the known world found themselves under Ottoman Rule. Islam threatened to take over Vienna. There was a shared sense that the church as an institution was at fault, failing at faithfulness, and there was a clear appetite for significant reform. The result was several different streams of protest movements in churches and regions, some of which eventually broke away from the Roman Church.

The gap between what church law stipulated and how people actually lived was obvious to many, and the leaders of reform movements were quick

---

1. Martin Luther, in a letter to nuns leaving their convents. *Luther: Letters of Spiritual Counsel*, 271.

to condemn the scandal of unfaithful celibates amongst the clergy and in the monasteries. It may have been a view that had held for more than a millennium, but as far as the reformers were concerned, celibacy was not the "better way": it was a special grace given by God to some people, but when attempted by those without such grace, it was an unbiblical, unchristian practice. Indeed, one of the earliest writings of the reformer Martin Luther was on celibacy: he argued that only the very few were fit for it, and that most people should embrace marriage as the *natural* way of life.

Luther looms especially large in this call to return to the "natural": "Marriage exists in all nature," he wrote, "for among all creatures there is the male and the female."[2] His own life story is an illustration of the same conviction: having renounced his own monastic vows, he married a former Cistercian nun, Katharina von Bora. Under Luther's direction, new homes were found for countless monks and nuns who wanted to start secular and married lives.

With his background as an Augustinian monk, Luther made the same connection as Augustine between sexual intercourse and original sin. However, he believed that most people simply could not withstand the force of sexual urges: "Before Adam fell it was a simple matter to remain virgin and chaste, but now it is hardly possible, and without special grace from God, quite impossible. For this very reason neither Christ nor the apostles sought to make chastity a matter of obligation."[3] Marriage was the appropriate way to channel the lust and limit the damage. And while it belonged to the temporal world, in Luther's understanding, marriage was not just for producing children, but also for sharing and enjoying human companionship. For our purposes, it is also important to note the move to the Old Testament as the basis of formulating this new theology of marriage: for Luther and for others, it was the estate ordained by God in Genesis.

In contrast to the Catholic teaching, Luther and most other reformers believed that marriage was not a sacrament—instead it was a contract, and as such it was to be regulated by the state rather than the church. Yet, although Protestantism seemingly lowered the status of marriage by removing its sacramental status, in practical terms marriage was elevated higher than ever before in the history of Christianity: it became "the cornerstone of society, the institution on which all other institutions were based."[4] It is also telling

2. Karant-Nunn and Wiesner-Hanks, *Luther on Women*, 122.

3. Luther, "A Sermon on the Estate of Marriage (1519)," in Lull and Russell, *Martin Luther's Basic Theological Writings*, 388.

4. Wiesner-Hanks, *Christianity and Sexuality*, 63.

that the seventeenth-century Puritans would call the marital home "a little commonwealth" and "a little Church."[5]

Unsurprisingly, such a view contributed to an atmosphere of suspicion towards single people, especially women: they were a cause for temptation and disruption of good societal order.[6] The reformers "made a clean sweep of the old families of strangers, including the village guilds, confraternities, and pilgrimage groups, leaving only the godly household in place."[7] In the reformed lands, celibacy became a rarity, and while men had an option or two for an alternative family structure in trade, the military, or education, for the unmarried women the opportunities swiftly closed down.[8] It is not by chance that nuns resisted the abolishment of their monastic houses much more strongly than monks: the latter could become priests, marry, or take up a secular trade, whereas nuns lost their spiritual vocation and the freedom for learning and leadership many of them had found in the convent.[9]

Another of the reformers, Jean Calvin, also described himself as being "hostile to celibacy."[10] In his younger years, he was not sure if he himself should marry, and surmised that if he were to marry, "it would be in order to devote my time to the Lord, by being the more relieved from the worries of daily life."[11] Yet, perhaps unsurprisingly, Calvin did eventually marry, choosing as his wife one Idelette de Bure, the widow of an Anabaptist, who already had two children. In his later years, he came to see marriage as a kind of a sacred covenant made in the sight of God (and in public), and an essential aspect of godly society. Ideally, such a covenant was not to be broken, but certain conditions and cases of hard fault, such as adultery or desertion, were recognized as warranting a divorce. Similar provisions appeared in the laws of a number of newly reformed countries. Given the fallen state of the world, reformers reasoned, some marriages were bound to end in divorce, and if a companionate marriage was no longer possible, then it was better that in such cases people were allowed to have their marriage dissolved.

The kind of reformation of the church that was propelled by such reformers as Luther and Calvin is generally known as the Magisterial Reformation.

---

5. These phrases were penned by William Gouge, and have been explored in Demos, *Little Commonwealth*. They also contain interesting echoes of the same image of family as "little church" by Chrysostom, a much earlier Eastern theologian.

6. Wiesner-Hanks, *Christianity and Sexuality*, 62.

7. Gillis, *World of Their Own Making*, 29–30.

8. Gillis, *World of Their Own Making*, 30.

9. Ruether, *Christianity and the Making of the Modern Family*, 70.

10. Wendel, *Calvin*, 65.

11. Wendel, *Calvin*, 65.

One of its features was an assumption that it shared with the institutional church all throughout the Christendom: namely, that church leadership should have a close relationship with the state. But, of course, that is not the whole story of the Reformation. A whole wing, usually referred to as the "Radical Reformation," held a different view: the majority of them believed that the church should neither be accountable to the state nor seek to dictate to the state, and that one's religion could not be enforced by the powers that be or even by one's own family. Yet at the same time, this was not an individualistic take on the faith, and nowhere is this clearer than in the Radical Reformers' view on marriage. It was not simply a matter between the couple intending to marry, or a concern of their parents. Rather, it was a question for a wider family—that of the true church of believers and followers of Christ. It is to their understanding of blood and marriage bonds that we turn next.

God's Family First: Anabaptists, Marriage, and Family

> Annelein received permission
> To see her son in Rotterdam,
> As her death drew near.
> Isaiah hear my testament,
> My last will before my death
> Now comes from my mouth.
>
> I am going on the path of the prophets,
> The martyrs' and apostles' way;
> There is none better.
> They all have drunk from the cup,
> Even as did Christ Himself,
> As I have heard it read.[12]

The eighteenth hymn in the Swiss Brethren Hymnal, *Ausbund*, tells the story of Annelein or Anna Jans, a twenty-eight-year-old widow with a fifteen-month-old son, who was brought before Rotterdam city officials to be tried and executed by drowning. The reason? She and her sister-in-Christ, Christiana Michiel Barents, had been overheard singing an Anabaptist hymn and consequently charged with sectarianism. Having confessed their faith, they

---

12. "Another Martyr Song," 345.

both met their death. The *Ausbund* tells the story of how Anna asked if anyone in the crowd would adopt her son, Esaias, or Isaiah.

Little Esaias grew up to become the mayor of Rotterdam—which is to say he did not become an Anabaptist. But the story and the song of Anna Jans poignantly highlights one of the key tenets of the Anabaptist faith: that there was a much greater reality of God's kingdom and the family of Jesus' followers, which was worth all the cost, including that of losing the nearest and dearest according to the flesh. Lest it give an impression of the lack of human emotion and attachment, here is another story. Jan Wouterss, another Anabaptist, wrote to his wife and daughter from prison, addressing his wife as "my dearest lamb," and telling her that "however much I loved you, I had to limit it, in order that if it should come to what it has now come, I might overcome the parting. Again, I loved my daughter rather more than I showed; I dared not set my affection too much upon her, in order that when I should have to part from her, as the Lord has ordered in regard to me, unworthy one, the bitter parting should not overcome me."[13]

At the heart of the Anabaptist faith was the desire to seek the same kind of radical re-evaluation of family bonds as taught by Jesus. As one historian notes, "[Anna] Jans and hundreds of others were killed precisely because they insisted that traditional assumptions regarding economics and politics and ethics and family life were not somehow written into the code of nature itself but could be refashioned in ways that would better reflect New Testament teachings and the example of Christ."[14]

One of the radical aspects of Anabaptism was a reconsideration of the woman's role, particularly in marriage. Rather than seeing their role primarily as that of submitting to their husbands, some Anabaptist women found their calling in teaching and public speaking, which often lead to their death. At times this caused serious marital disruption and public scandal. Mennonite theologian and historian Hans-Jürgen Goertz reports that a number of Anabaptist women abandoned their husbands if they were unwilling to join the Anabaptist cause. "Other women 'avoided' their husbands, dissolved their 'worldly' marriages and entered into 'spiritual' marital relations. Loyalty to God was more important than mere human ties."[15] Anabaptists also generally objected to what they saw as mixed marriages—that is, marrying someone who was not an Anabaptist.

This is not to say, however, that marriage did not matter: it was understood to be a spiritual reality and a spiritual union which was ordained by

13. Braght, "Fifth Letter," 913.
14. Roth, "Family, Community and Discipleship," 150.
15. Goertz, *Anabaptists*, 116.

God at the beginning and reflected the relationship between Christ and his body. But it was also firmly set in the context of the community of faith. Or as articulated in the *Martyrs Mirror*, a book of Anabaptist testimony:

> Of marriage we confess: That the same is honorable and an ordinance of God, who in the beginning instituted this state with the two human beings first created in the image of God, blessed it, and joined them together. . . . Hence, every believer who desires to enter into matrimony, must follow this doctrine of Christ and the above example, and unite himself in marriage only with one person, who has been, by a like faith with him, born from above, of God, and renewed, and created after the image of God. And such persons, after their parents and the church have given their consent, shall, in the presence of the church, with fervent prayer to God, be joined together by a minister.[16]

The Anabaptist understanding of the primacy of their church family was also reflected in their practice of shunning: that is, cutting ties with those who had abandoned the way of Jesus. Here is an excerpt from the writing of the leader of one of the Anabaptist groups, Menno Simons. In his argument for the use of shunning, Simons employs a potpourri of metaphors of marriage, family, *and* celibate singleness:

> For the church is a congregation of saints . . . and, as Adam had but one Eve, who was flesh of his flesh and bone of his bone, Isaac but one Rebecca, who was of his own family, and Christ but one body, which was heavenly and from heaven . . . ; thus has he also, spiritually, but one Eve, but one new Rebecca, who is his spiritual body, spouse, church and bride, namely, the believers, the regenerated, meek, merciful, dead to sin, righteous, peaceable, amicable and obedient children in his kingdom and house of peace; pure, chaste virgins in the Spirit, holy souls, who are of his divine family, and holy flesh of his flesh, and bone of his bone.
>
> From which, according to the doctrine of the holy apostles, it is evident that the obstinate disturber or sectary who causes . . . offence and discord . . . who lead an offensive life, or the over-curious, inquisitive and lazy, who live at the expense of others, shall not be suffered in the holy house . . . but that we . . . should exclude and shun them, according to Scripture, to *our*, salvation, and *their* reformation. Faithful children, be you warned.[17]

---

16. "Article XXV," 401.

17. Simons, *Complete Works*, 246.

The shunning would have been carried out by the whole community, including the immediate family of the offender. It was never a private arrangement—as indeed was true of many other aspects of Anabaptist practice of marriage and family. At least some of the Anabaptist congregations had a say in such matters as the financial dealings of a particular family, and could forbid gaining money by, say, speculation or lending money for interest.[18] Such aspects of early Anabaptist life are reminders that "the church—not the biological family—[was to be] the primary point of reference for social, religious, ethical and economic identity."[19]

It is important to note here that particularities of the teaching and practice varied considerably amongst different Anabaptist streams. A rather different approach to marriage was worked out in the city of Muenster which was ruled by a group of radical Anabaptists between 1534 and 1535. Given that women outnumbered men by three times in Muenster, perhaps they have reached the most straightforward solution: polygyny, or one man marrying several wives.[20] To defend this solution, Muenster Anabaptists appealed to the fact that it was an accepted practice in much of the Old Testament, and of which there was no explicit condemnation in the Bible.

One important aspect of polygamy was its potential to take care of "unattached" and therefore vulnerable people in a collective society with limited resources, and it could be argued that it was reflected in Muenster men's sometimes marrying older wives who clearly were not able to bear children. On the other hand, it may also have been the most convenient way of exercising control over women who otherwise would have had a much freer, if more precarious, life in those chaotic days of attempted theocracy.[21]

Muenster Anabaptists differed from their namesakes elsewhere in their approach to the use of force and the separation of the church from the world. Instead, their attempt to reorder the whole of society meant making marriage central to their worldview and reorganizing community life around it. Our context today may seem to be worlds apart, but I do wonder whether we do not live under the same temptation. This would not necessarily be the temptation of polygamy, but that of capitulating to the powerful draw of making marriage, or the nuclear family, the organizing principle of our lives. However, this discussion will need to await another chapter.

The temptation to give up the vision of the church as one's primary family also accompanied the Anabaptist experience, as illustrated by the story of

18. Roth, "Family, Community and Discipleship," 151.
19. Roth, "Family, Community and Discipleship," 152.
20. Jelsma, *Frontiers of the Reformation*, 68.
21. Grieser, "Tale of Two Convents," 32.

later Mennonite communities. In the midst of persecutions, the second and third generations often found themselves relying on the support of their immediate and extended families. Given their separation, both chosen and enforced, from the wider culture, family and church often became inseparable, and much of that radical idea of the church as the new family was lost.[22] At the very least, this leaves us with as a reminder that the radical nature of Jesus' call needs to be rediscovered and lived out by each generation anew.

Marriage and Singleness in Modernity

> Before they settled on what we now think of as the Victorian family, Americans and Europeans tried out a wide range of communal and spiritual options. . . . New father and mother figures rose to meet the need for security and continuity, and people broke with their flesh and blood, not in opposition to religion but in its name, to find shelter in the spiritual families created by the religious revivals that coursed across North America and Europe.[23]

Though unusual among the Anabaptists, the Muenster experiment of polygyny was not the last. The early nineteenth century was a particularly vibrant time for religious revivals as well as various alternatives to conventional marriage arrangements or single household living. One of the best known of these is Joseph Smith's movement of the Latter Day Saints, or Mormonism, and its embrace of plural marriage, but there were a number of other similar attempts to shape community life around "complex marriage," such as John Humphrey Noyes' Oneida Community in New York, marked by its communal responsibility for children. There were also similar secular visions: Robert Owen, a Welsh social reformer, thought that conventional marriage was nothing natural, and advocated communal sharing of housing, meals, and education as a better version of extended family life. In the mid-1820s, he took these ideas on a journey from his textile factory town in New Lanark, Scotland across the Atlantic to found a short-lived experiment in utopian socialism in New Harmony, in the US state of Indiana.

Some other communities, however, went the opposite way and built their common life on the basis of celibacy. The memory of one such religious community still lingers today—mostly through the legacy of their kitchen cabinetry style. Its founder was an abused wife, Anne Lee, who lost all four of her children in infancy, and came to regard "marriage of the flesh" as "a

22. Roth, "Family, Community and Discipleship," 152.

23. Gillis, *World of Their Own Making*, 66.

covenant with death and an agreement with Hell."[24] Founded in the mid-eighteenth century in England, but really establishing themselves in the United States, the Shakers practiced celibate communal living. Egalitarian and with a key role played by several women leaders, the Shakers' key tenets echoed those of the earlier centuries' communities: sexual abstinence was associated with paradise or an angelic state (and conversely sexual intercourse with the fall). However, their community also often included children—those of converts, or those who were orphaned or abandoned and had nowhere else to turn.

Such movements and experiments appeared in the midst of immense changes triggered by the Industrial Revolution. As with other times in history marked by upheaval, traditional norms no longer felt steady; new ways of organizing life suddenly seemed possible. Attempts to rethink family life resulted in the multiplication of associations and friendly societies, many of which envisioned themselves as brothers and sisters.[25] Sexual values and practices were also changing, particularly during what some scholars refer to as the "sexual" (rather than industrial) revolution of mid-eighteenth to mid-nineteenth centuries. Changing economic conditions and social conventions gave greater freedom in the socializing between the sexes, and out-of-wedlock pregnancies skyrocketed.[26]

As before, a considerable proportion of people stayed unmarried for all or a great part of their lives: farm hands, servants, members of religious communities, some radical thinkers who opposed marriage in principle, and so on. The case of the so-called "surplus women" in mid-Victorian Britain is particularly interesting: the census of 1851 revealed that there were half a million more women than men, and two and a half million women were not married. The reaction to this news was a moral panic about the decline of marriage and family norms, and the impact that these "redundant" women would have on the society as a whole.[27] No matter how many of them were around, working single women were treated as an anomaly; as one of the periodicals of the time put it, "Married life is woman's profession. . . . Of course, by not getting a husband, or losing him, she may find she is without resources. All that can be said of her is, she has failed in business and no social reform can prevent such failures."[28]

As the production of goods moved away from the traditional family home, another revolution was taking place: rather than being part of one's

24. Quoted in Gillis, *World of Their Own Making*, 68.

25. Gillis, *World of Their Own Making*, 67.

26. Bowring, *Erotic Love*, 92.

27. Levitan, "Redundancy," 363.

28. "Queen Bees or Working Bees," 576.

livelihood and community, marriage and family were increasingly centering around the concept of romantic love and individual choice, resulting in a very particular image of an "ideal family." It may not have been immediately obvious, but it gradually developed into a powerful ideology under the shadow of which we continue to live even today.

The Victorian Family:
The Romance of Coupledom and Parenthood

> Middle-class Victorians turned the family into an object of worshipful contemplation. As a result of the crisis of faith that had caused so many to have serious doubts about the existence of God and his transcendent order, the family became proof of the existence of the divine. . . . Victorians on both sides of the Atlantic began to worship God through their families.[29]

Rather than any earlier family model, contemporary supporters of "family values" still turn to the picture of Victorian family, appealing to it as a representation of a God-given order for Christians. Arising out of mid-1800s middle-class Britain, this "nostalgic imagination as a normative model" spread throughout the Western world. In many ways, it signaled the surrender of the hope of a godly society, and instead embraced a much more modest goal of the pious privacy of home.[30]

As it kept shedding its productive functions, the family home became the center of such values as emotional fulfillment and prestige. That is not to say that the lives of most people were anything like prestigious. The icon of an ideal family being presented did not have much in common with the reality of many families going through high child mortality, surviving spousal deaths, and living in mixed households of subsequent marriages. But the model, solidified in the representation of middle-class family life, was to become an ideal to strive for, whatever one's class. Once available, family photographs became the postures of this ideal. Various symbols were increasingly employed to consolidate a sense of "our family," such as household objects which now were primarily marked not by their economic, but their sentimental value.[31]

As we will see later, at the core of this new family world was the story of romantic love. Romance had a particular significance for the woman, and

---

29. Gillis, *World of Their Own Making*, 71.

30. Ruether, *Christianity and the Making of the Modern Family*, 102–3.

31. Gillis, *World of Their Own Making*, 75–76.

the wedding became "the foremost female rite of passage. The groom stepped into the background, allowing the bride to occupy the center of attention."[32] Bound by their love, the husband and the wife were to live in an intense rapport between themselves and the children. Rather than being a part and parcel of a larger framework, such as joining in a common work or community celebrations, intimate relationships and family occasions now carried an explicit value in and of themselves.

While broadcasting its public image, the family became privatized as never before. Amidst increasing individualism and religious skepticism, it began to take over the functions previously fulfilled by community and religion. Home was no longer simply the roof over one's head, shared with various people who may or may not be one's relatives. Rather, the home and the hearth became a sanctuary of sorts: "a magic circle of pure womanhood and innocent childhood, an unfallen garden of Eden set against a sinful male realm of business and politics."[33] This is not to say, of course, that the Victorian family was meant to replace institutionalized religion: for a long time, the two were considered two sides of the same coin. But the church was increasingly seen to exist in order to support the life of the family, rather than the other way around.[34]

The role of the woman as a wife and mother is particularly illustrative of the Victorian version of marriage and family. While in pre-modern times, the work of both husband and wife was directed at maintaining the economic productivity of their unit, within this new model the wife's domestic work was generating and upholding "the rituals, myths, and images on which the newly enchanted world of family had come to depend."[35] This has remained the woman's responsibility even after a momentous shift, at a later stage, from wife as a homemaker to a working wife and mother. Even as an equal breadwinner, or indeed even in the case of being the sole bread-winner with an unemployed partner, the woman is likely to still be seen as the major contributor to the "making of the family."

The notion of motherhood also underwent a major shift. Let us recall that in medieval Christianity, spiritual families were generally rated much higher than biological, "earthly" families, and spiritual motherhood, such as in the monastic context, generally tended to be prized much more than physical childbearing.[36] In social terms, taking care of children had often

32. Gillis, *World of Their Own Making*, 146.

33. Ruether, *Christianity and the Making of the Modern Family*, 103.

34. Ruether, *Christianity and the Making of the Modern Family*, 104.

35. Gillis, *World of Their Own Making*, 77.

36. Atkinson, *Oldest Vocation*, 239–40.

been shared between the whole household. Now, however, motherhood was increasingly defined by the biological function. In this new world, its novels and its newspaper editorials, the mother became the central and saintly figure of the family home. Although the father was still the head of the family, he was in many senses displaced: home was the mother's domain.

That said, giving birth did nothing to sanctify mothers in dire poverty or slavery. Family hearth may have been represented as the center of one's life, but countless families were living in slums, forced to sell their children into enslaved labor or prostitution. More than that: whatever the class, the Victorian family model was an ideal behind which to hide the reality: "the spectacle of intimacy, the wild efflorescence in the public signs, traces, slogans, and figures of domesticity, until it was scarcely possible to see the home beneath the mottoes enshrining it."[37] While romance and companionate marriage were extoled as the standard to uphold, this took place in the shadow of the rampant spread of venereal diseases. Cohabitation was widespread, not in the least because obtaining divorce was impossible for many until well into the twentieth century. And numbers suggest that while not exactly desirable, unmarried motherhood was more acceptable than we often imagine.[38]

The twentieth century saw the Victorian family ideal shaken and battered by wars, radical political movements, the massive employment of women, effective contraception, and the sexual revolution of the 1960s. However, it also received a powerful boost in the "golden age" of the nuclear family in the 1950s, when the post-war consumer revolution turned marriage into a universal standard. This was particularly true for the United States, where marriage came to be regarded "as the only culturally acceptable route to adulthood and independence."[39] During the same decade, reference to "traditional marriage" became established in the way we know it today: the husband as a provider, the wife as a homemaker, their union born out of and sustained by the romance of love. What is often forgotten is how high divorce rates were during this "golden age." Before too long, social attitudes in the West changed dramatically. Cohabitation soared, divorce rates continued to rise, and single parenthood became increasingly socially acceptable. And so we find ourselves in the current world that was described in the first pages of this book: the growing diversity of family forms and the recurrent calls to address the "family crisis" as blended families become mainstream, more and more countries legalize gay marriage, and an increasing proportion of people stay single.

37. Chase and Levenson, *Spectacle of Intimacy*, 215.
38. Thane, *Happy Families?*, 20–21.
39. Coontz, *Marriage*, 230.

Although the changes over the past few decades have been radical indeed, it is important to keep in mind that the sense of a "crisis" or a "disintegration of the family" leading to a "disintegration of society" seems to accompany humanity throughout its history. Pat Thane, a British historian, also draws attention to the fact that, regardless of the historical era, it is the poorest who struggle most to maintain stable life, and that therefore "socio-economic inequality may be a more important challenge than features of the family itself." This is yet another reminder of the mythical nature of the "traditional" family: "There was no golden age, when the mass of the population lived contentedly in long-lasting, stable, two-parent nuclear families, extra-marital sex and family violence were almost unheard of and most older people were nurtured by adult children more prosperous than they."[40]

Yet the Victorian family ideal has proven to be extraordinarily persistent, surviving even through the radical shifts of societies which now understand themselves as secular.[41] Even new family forms reflect the power of this model as they, too, embrace "the power of love" and its expression in marriage.[42] What is its allure, and why is it so passionately invoked today as the "traditional" (and in the view of some, the "biblical") family model?[43]

Even after the seismic shifts of the last century and the radical changes in societal attitudes towards different family forms, the model continues to function as the embodiment of ordinary human happiness, whether within or outside the confines of marriage. In the next chapter will see how our Western cultures, our churches, and each one of us personally live under the master story of coupled love: individuals brought and bound together by the power of romance, finding in it their happiness and shelter from the big bad world.

40. Thane, *Happy Families?*, 67.

41. Atkinson, *Oldest Vocation*, 243.

42. E.g., "Power of Love."

43. We may also note that it continues to play a key part in the wider ideology of individualism, an assumption of liberal market and capitalist organization of society as the best, and a view that the nuclear family is the basic, and natural, element for social stability and healthy progress.

7

"And They Lived Happily Ever After"

The Obligation of Coupled Love

The link between the words "romantic love" and "happiness" is a good way to capture the shift in the understanding of marriage which continues to shape our culture today. In many ways, its roots can be traced back to the Enlightenment and the beginning of the "pursuit of happiness." Which, of course, is not to say that happiness was of no interest before: from Aristotle's explorations of human flourishing—*eudaimonia*—to Augustine's reflection on the human search for happiness, to Thomas Aquinas' thoughts on the bliss of eternity, as humans we have been thinking about happiness for a very long time. But over the last couple of centuries, the focus on happiness has come to the fore like never before. Increasingly, people started being "concerned about [their] happiness the way people before [them] had been concerned about the salvation of their souls."[1] Their understanding of the sources of happiness also shifted radically. Happiness has become an assumed goal and an implicit standard by which our lives are judged—a significant burden to carry when being less than "happy" is considered to be a failure. But before we look at the prevailing norms of happiness in our culture today, we need to consider, briefly, the evolution of the concept of romantic love and its relationship to marriage and happiness.

---

1. Bruckner, *Perpetual Euphoria*, 1.

Love and Marriage, Horse and Carriage

> Marriage as an institution may seem to be on the rocks, but romantic love has never been more valued than right now. . . . Establishing a romantic relationship with another person, of different or same sex, is the sign of adulthood in modern Western culture. Yet all of this is a recent development, for it was not really until the [nineteenth] century that the perfect couple assumed a central place in the Western imagination.[2]

As we have already seen, it was the Victorian family model that proved to be a fertile soil for the romantic basis of marital choice and marital life. However, the Victorian passion for romance did not spring out of nowhere, and in order to understand how romance became such a central aspect of marriage, we need to go a little further back, to eleventh- and twelfth-century Europe. A time of one of the most extensive religious reforms, popular piety, and asceticism, this period witnessed a curious outburst of an interest in stories of courtly love. Immortalized in the literary fashion of chivalric romance, this love followed a particular script: a knight performing mighty deeds for the sake of his noble lady—typically the wife of his superior—adoring her, defending her honor, and proving his love through deeds of valor.[3] This was "pure love," with strong religious overtones. Here is how one of the troubadour songwriters, Giraut de Borneil, sang about it:

> For Love burns and constrains me;
> And if it was once remote and distant from me
> Now that I turn and aspire [to this lady]
> It will be fitting for me to submit to its ensign
> And to scorn all others.[4]

Fascination with love as perpetual desire "became a full-fledged shadow religion with a morality and a ritual all its own . . . offering lovers a justification for coming together safe from the prying eyes of priests and jealous husbands."[5] Importantly, though, the medieval romance did not end in a happy marriage, or a happy outcome of any other sort. It was not a livable kind of love: by definition it was doomed for suffering. Its perfect consummation was found in the death of the lovers, through which fulfilment and deliverance were achieved:

2. Gillis, *World of Their Own Making*, 133.

3. See, e.g., Porter, *Courtly Love*.

4. Quoted in Reddy, *Making of Romantic Love*, 153.

5. Reddy, *Making of Romantic Love*, 167.

think of Tristan and Isold, Aucassin and Nicolette, Romeo and Juliet, and other stars of medieval literature. Or consider a real-life embodiment of the tragic nature of romantic love that has fascinated the Western imagination ever since: Abelard and Heloise, two brilliant twelfth-century thinkers, who fell in love with each other while Abelard was Heloise's tutor. Having borne him a son, Heloise ended up in a secret marriage with Abelard, but their lives were radically changed after Abelard was assaulted and castrated by Heloise's relatives. They both entered religious orders, and their correspondence over the following decades, while touching upon a wide array of subjects, carries the memory of the passionate love they once shared. In the words of Heloise herself, "Of all wretched women I am the most wretched, and amongst the unhappy I am unhappiest. The higher I was exalted when you preferred me to all other women, the greater my suffering over my own fall and yours, when equally I was flung down; for the higher the ascent, the heavier the fall."[6]

Stories like these provided the background for how the Western world came to approach human love.[7] Scholars continue to debate the precise nuances and developments of the medieval romance, but its impact on our Western culture is unquestionable. American literary critic R. Howard Bloch argues that the medieval romance has given us our "notion of romantic fascination that governs what we say about love, what we say to the ones we love, what we expect them to say to us, . . . how we act and expect them to act, how we negotiate our relation to the social—in short, the hygiene that governs our erotic imagination."[8] Even those who hold to a more skeptical—or, they may say, more realistic—view of human love are living in the world which assumes the centrality and the power of romantic love and its power "as a spell, terror, or ideal."[9]

As they evolved, the expectations and the clichés of romantic love underwent various modifications. During the Victorian age, romantic love enthusiastically moved into marriage, and was no longer to be necessarily terminated by some kind of a tragedy. The anguish of romance was increasingly limited to the time of courtship, during which the lovers were to overcome their obstacles and conflicts: this is how one earned one's future happiness. The earlier scripts of romance were significantly modified by an explosion of a new kind of literature: the romantic novel. Consumed widely and eagerly, these books established a new kind of narrative of love, in which romance was both inescapable and particular: "they were meant for each other" and they

6. Abelard and Heloise, *Letters of Abelard and Heloise*, 65.

7. Reddy, *Making of Romantic Love*, 2.

8. Bloch, *Medieval Misogyny*, 8–9.

9. Rougemont, *Love in the Western World*, 23.

"fell" in love. Although its style has changed significantly since the Victorian era, the romantic novel continued to thrive, even through an increasing sexualization of romance. It is still particularly geared towards women, but now caters to all tastes: straight, gay and lesbian, historical, contemporary, "science fiction, erotic, paranormal" or "inspirational" (that is, conservative Christian romance fiction).[10]

In fact, the idea that human beings cannot help but be looking for "their other half" is as old as Plato's *Symposium*. In the book, comic playwright Aristophanes recounts the story of the origins of love. Human beings, he explains, have actually been split into two by the gods, and ever since they have been searching for their missing half: "I believe that if our loves were perfectly accomplished, and each one returning to his primeval nature had his original true love, then our race would be happy."[11] The Victorian romantic novel took up Aristophanes' tale with enthusiasm, establishing it as a permanent feature of our modern cultural imagination: love is to be the cure for the wound of separation that we all carry.[12] Thus we speak of a spouse as "one's other half," and people search for their "soulmate" destined just for them so persistently that this search can become a duty: unless they find their "True Love," they will have failed.[13] The idea of the passionate search for one's missing half is also easily found in today's churches, as we shall see later, in the implicit notion that one should marry "the one (and only) given by God." Hence the agony of those not sure if the person they are dating (or, worse still, have already married) indeed is "the one."

Indeed, this romantic script goes far beyond the confines of a book: it pervades the globalized cultural air we breathe. The grammar of romantic love is learned alongside learning our first language. "The happily-in-love, pair-bonded (generally, although increasingly not exclusively, heterosexual) couple is made into a near mandatory norm by the media and popular culture, as this romance story is endlessly taught and replayed in a multiplicity of cultural sites: Disney princess movies, the wedding industry, fairytales, Hollywood movies, pop music lyrics, advertising, the diamond jewelry industry, and more."[14] Although it is increasingly challenged by alternative incarnations of romance, marriage still claims its central place in the story of a happy coupledom. A surprising and dramatic marriage proposal, the diamonds on the ring, and the "perfect wedding" are the central props for the script of "marrying

10. Roach, *Happily Ever After*, 6–7.

11. Plato, *Symp.*

12. Bowring, *Erotic Love*, 111.

13. Roach, *Happily Ever After*, 26.

14. Roach, *Happily Ever After*, 4.

true love"—even though, apparently, the more expensive the engagement ring and wedding, the greater the chance of a divorce.[15] Yet even amidst high divorce rates and widespread cohabitation, "the perfect wedding" continues to capture our cultural imagination and loosen our purse strings.

Similarly to the strongly religious connotations of the medieval romance, researchers note the same about contemporary Western love scripts: "Romance functions as a religious belief system offering guidance on the end goal of how to live a worthy life."[16] Love is "one main source of satisfaction and meaning in life. [It is our new] religion after religion, the ultimate belief after the end of all faith."[17] However, this religion of romantic love requires no exclusivity, and can attach itself to a profession of any particular religion. It can quite cozily settle within Christian culture. It is thus that the relationship between God and a believer—individualized to the core—can be described in romantic terms in worship songs. But even more importantly, God's ultimate blessing is associated with the gift of a romantic partner, leading, of course, to a happy marriage.

However, this hoped-for happiness has a shadowy side. The religion of romantic love inhabits a zone of tension between the expectation of salvation and the acknowledgement of a possible failure. When brought into marital expectations, love as romance finds itself under enormous pressure by a long-term prospect and the practicalities of the mundane life. Indeed, if one marries for romantic feelings only, then it can easily follow that one does not have to *stay* in marriage if such feelings disappear. Rather than being a singular life-changing event, romance can be repeated and recreated in each new act of "falling in love."

The increasing availability of divorce has made serial marriage easier than ever before. Moreover, the social acceptability of cohabitation has made it possible for people to be looking for their "one true love" and the "happily ever after" without even having to go through the trouble of formal marriage.[18] Note, however, that such an endless pursuit of romantic love risks remaining largely content-less: as Rodney Clapp notes, "romantic love cannot even provide us with a description of 'ever after.'"[19] And so we turn now to consider the

---

15. Francis-Tan and Mialon, "Diamond is Forever."

16. Roach, *Happily Ever After*, 17.

17. Beck and Beck-Gernsheim, quoted in Bowring, *Erotic Love*, 225.

18. As noted in the Introduction, my usage of the word *marriage* in a contemporary sense includes any long-term, committed practice of coupledom, whether formal or not, whatever may be said of the theological significance of a religious ceremony or a legal recognition of such a bond.

19. Clapp, "From Family Values to Family Virtues," 198.

preoccupation with, and ideas about, happiness—a persistent feature of our current cultural climate.

Happiness: Meanings and Relationships

> As I reflect on what I mean when I say my life is or is not happy, I see that I have judgments in mind about myself, the world, what is satisfying now and over the long term, what is worth pursuing and avoiding, and so forth.[20]

First of all, what do we mean when we talk of "happiness"? It is such a slippery word, meaning different things to different people in different contexts. "Are you happy now?" may be a question asked after someone finally gets an ice cream they have been demanding on a hot summer's afternoon. "Only in God (or having children, or serving our country) can we find happiness" is a claim of a different caliber. The talk of being "happy" in a psychological sense is yet of another kind, as is a consideration of the chemical balance of the body and its effect on moods, perceptions, and emotions. Further still, researchers discuss objective measurements of happiness in different societies on the basis of economic and social factors. We could also ask whether happiness is a state or a process. Is it about fulfilment, or is it really even more about longing—in the observation of Winnie the Pooh, the *anticipation* of eating honey, rather than its actual consumption? Or, as others would suggest, is happiness only possible when it is not chased? Whole books are devoted to detailed discussions of various definitions and approaches.[21] However, there is an overall sense common to them all: it is about having or living a good life, or even the best life, whether it be termed "quality of life," "life satisfaction," "wellbeing," or "fulfilment," "flourishing," and "meaningful life."[22]

Secondly, *what* is it that is supposed to make people happy? Dan Haybron, a happiness scholar, provides the following summary:

> There is no definitive list of the main sources of happiness . . . partly because it is not clear how to divide them up. But the following items seem generally to be accepted as among the chief correlates of happiness: relationships, engagement in interesting and challenging activities, material and physical security, a sense of

20. Griswold, "Happiness, Tranquillity, and Philosophy," 15.

21. See, for instance, David et al., *Oxford Handbook of Happiness*.

22. One may note here two rather distinct approaches to happiness: the first one is concerned with the current experience of positive mental and emotional state, whereas the second one looks at one's life development as a whole.

meaning or purpose, a positive outlook, and autonomy or control. Significant correlates may also include—among many others—religion, good governance, trust, helping others, values (e.g., having non-materialistic values), achieving goals, not being unemployed, and perhaps also connection with the natural environment.[23]

Of course, one of the difficulties here is correlation: are these the reasons or conditions for happiness, or its outcomes? Do we feel happy because we enjoy loving relationships with others, or does our own life satisfaction lead us to acquiring and maintaining successful bonds with other people? Whatever the case may be, note that relationships tend to sit at the top of the list of predictors of happiness. It is not difficult to see why: humans are social beings in the need of close and meaningful social connections—a fact that has been highlighted by the current "epidemic of loneliness" which is now considered to be a global health issue.[24] Research consistently draws attention to the fact that, across different cultures, "being in a close relationship, the number of close relationships one has, and the quality of relationship experiences in general, are robust and consistent correlates of happiness."[25]

"Relationships" is a broad category, but happiness studies have primarily focused on coupled relationships, with much less interest in other family members and friends.[26] Just occasionally, attention is drawn to other bonds, such as friendships, even though when studies are carried out, they tend to find that "friendship experiences . . . are an essential, consistent, and robust correlate of happiness across the lifespan and across cultures."[27] But most of the time, romantic and sexual bonds get the limelight of happiness research. Marriage is often simply assumed to provide for better quality relationships than a single lifestyle: "The mere fact of being married has been repeatedly linked to happiness, irrespective of the quality of the marital relationship"; or, as the title of one book suggests, *Why Married People are Happier, Healthier, and Better off Financially.*[28]

And of course, it is not difficult to see the reasoning behind treating coupledom as a staple of human happiness. Economic and emotional benefits of marriage seem quite obvious to many (although whether marriage makes one happier or being happier makes marriage more likely has been much less

23. Haybron, "Happiness," 3.3.

24. See, for instance, Ortiz-Ospina and Roser, "Loneliness and Social Connections."

25. Demir, "Introduction to Relationships and Happiness," 877.

26. Demir, "Introduction to Relationships and Happiness," 879.

27. Demir et al., "Friendship and Happiness," 928.

28. Saphire-Bernstein and Taylor, "Close Relationships," 884; Waite and Gallagher, *Case for Marriage.*

explored).[29] Here, for example, is a statement by Richard Layard, a popular economist and happiness researcher: "People generally become happier as a result of marriage. . . . The main benefits of marriage or cohabitation are obvious: you give each other love and comfort; you share resources, gaining economies of scale; you help each other. Married people also have better sex lives. . . . Furthermore, married people are healthier and live longer."[30]

Nevertheless, as we shall see later, single people may actually maintain more, not less, significant and deep relationships: intimate friendships, sibling ties, and close bonds formed through their involvement in intentional communities.[31] All of these links significantly contribute to a person's wellbeing, yet are often dismissed as somehow less important, and less meaningful, than the support of nuclear family and particularly the spouse or partner. Thus we see again how much the whole society is still shaped by the idea—indeed, an ideology—of marriage as the key source of individual happiness and fulfilment.[32] While some social scientists draw attention to a high degree of stereotyping and unchecked assumptions in scientific studies on single and partnered people, the unquestioned correlation of marriage and happiness continues to inform the media, public policies, and the work of the researchers themselves.[33]

The Pressure Cooker of Coupled Happiness

> Today, we turn to one person to provide what an entire village once did: a sense of grounding, meaning, and continuity. At the same time, we expect our committed relationships to be romantic as well as emotionally and sexually fulfilling. Is it any wonder that so many relationships crumble under the weight of it all?[34]

There is, however, an enormous elephant in the room. If marriage is such a significant source of a happy life, then why is divorce so prevalent? Here is an interesting fact. While people self-report an increase of happiness at the start of marriage or a committed living together, before too long those happiness

---

29. Stutzer and Frey, "Does Marriage Make People Happy."

30. Layard, *Happiness*, loc. 1060, 1071.

31. DePaulo and Morris, "Singles in Society and in Science," 71–72.

32. I argue this in more detail in Andronovienė, *Transforming the Struggles*, chapters 3 and 5.

33. DePaulo and Morris, "Singles in Society and in Science," 65–80.

34. Perel, *Mating in Captivity*, xiv.

levels return to the personal default position.[35] In fact, "part of the increase in happiness or life satisfaction that appears to be the result of being married may be due to the fact that married individuals feel that they have successfully met these cultural expectations—they have succeeded in this aspect of their lives."[36] We have yet to see what role the slow waning of marriage as cultural norm will have upon these expectations. For now, however, the linking of marriage to happiness continues to dominate cultural assumptions and life patterns.

Here again we are reminded how much the married couple's relationship has been removed from the larger, communal fabric. No one is supposed to be told whom to marry, so it is up to the individual to make sure the relationship is a "happy" one: an enormous freedom, but also an enormous personal responsibility. British sociologist Anthony Giddens describes the contemporary ideal of the romantic bond as a "pure relationship": freed from reproductive purposes, gender inequalities, and economic necessities, it is to last only as long as it is fulfilling to both partners.[37]

Largely stripped of other ties that previously bound the partners to the various members of the extended family and their community, the pressure of having a truly happy marriage can easily become too much to bear. As philosopher and theologian Diogenes Allen observes, we live with "unrealistic expectations [which] make it impossible for the institution of marriage to provide the blessings it *can* offer." He continues:

> We expect our spouse to be a friend, indeed, to be our best friend. This may happen, but is it a requirement of marriage? In our confusion over the nature of friendship, we ask a spouse to be something we do not ask of friends. A spouse is to take an interest in everything a husband or wife does, but this contradicts the nature of friendship, which is based on freedom. As if this were not enough, parents are also required to participate in their children's interests. Then, on top of all this, marriage is supposed to allow us to realize our potential, enable us to grow, and not cut us off from any of life's interesting and desirable experiences. Is it surprising that people are disappointed with their marriages when their expectations are so demanding and contradictory?[38]

Compared to our predecessors, yet more pressure is added by today's increased life expectancy, with marriage potentially stretching for decades

35. E.g., Lucas and Clark, "Do People Really Adapt."
36. Wadsworth, "Marriage and Subjective Well-being," 1026.
37. Giddens, *Transformation of Intimacy.*
38. Allen, *Love*, 97.

after the children have left home. It is no coincidence that many "empty nesters" experience a serious possibility of a divorce: once the previous focus on raising children is removed from the family's daily activities, it can reveal two strangers struggling to perform the happy couple narrative.

Yet even when the risks, challenges, and the hard work involved in keeping a marriage alive and healthy are recognized, this recognition is often accompanied by an implicit belief that it is still much better than a life of singleness. Chapter 1 provided examples of how single people—even single people who by all accounts seem to be very happy—are persistently viewed with suspicion or pity: surely they cannot be as happy as they would be if they were married. It is almost as if happiness apart from marriage is not permitted; it is as if the presence of "happy singles" presents a threat to the hallowed narrative of romantic love's happiness, and an affront to the respectable happiness of coupledom. The idea of marital happiness does not seem to be able to even tolerate any alternatives.

Family Without a Partner: The Happiness of Parenting

> In the absence of a good partnership, and with the rate of divorce as high as it is, we believe, and research has shown, that being raised by a caring and competent single parent is definitely a viable option. . . . We have made a serious and thoughtful decision to take on the responsibility of raising a child by ourselves, and we have chosen not to bring a child into a relationship that is not a satisfactory one.[39]

But alternatives do exist. Here is one of the most common aspirations to happiness and fulfillment: parenthood. In the past, of course, parenthood was most intrinsically linked with the idea of coupling; in fact, as we have seen in the previous chapters, the whole purpose of marriage was so that parenthood could take place. And even today, happiness is most commonly associated with "having a family": that is, having both a romantic and sexual relationship, and children. The words of this anonymous forum commentator express it well: "A loving, meaningful relationship—and children also—is ultimately going to prove [most] fulfilling. . . . That's simply the way humans are hardwired and programmed and deep down (not that deep, really) everyone knows as much."[40] Yet the link between coupledom and children is no longer automatic.

---

39. An introduction to Single Mothers by Choice, an organization providing support for single motherhood. "Philosophy," 3.

40. Anonymous comment by TrolloMcTrollFace in Benincasa, "Psychologists Say."

For some, parenthood is a major source of fulfilled life quite apart from love interests or sexual fulfillment, because they have consciously chosen single parenting as their most important life goal. Others choose to focus on parenting after a major disappointment or fruitless search for romantic love.

However, just as with the pressure of finding lasting romance, parenthood can become an oppressive requirement in order to qualify for happiness; or to say it differently, "even in our progressive Western society, childlessness still carries a stigma."[41] This is especially true for women: "A modern woman is left with few doubts about her primary identity. She may be a wife, consort, helpmeet, and lover, but she is above all a mother," writes historian John Gillis.[42] The happiness-in-motherhood motif is particularly interesting because it is represented as the most natural and unquestionable sources of identity and fulfillment. Yet, as we saw earlier, just a few centuries ago motherhood was understood much more broadly, and was not necessarily connected with giving birth and nurturing one's own offspring. Wet-nurses, used not only by the upper-class but working mothers too, adults adopting their relatives' children or complete strangers, godparents, and monks were all understood to be doing "mothering."[43] But all of this has been almost entirely forgotten.

The happiness of a woman as mother comes with a price: one is supposed to be a good—an *ideal*—mother. The job description for this role can be frighteningly demanding, and the sense of failure immense. As Gillis sums it up, "Never [before] have mothers been so burdened by motherhood."[44] In reaction to such high expectations, some women are opting for a childfree life. Of course, other factors also play a role: one's career, the presence or stability of an intimate relationship, financial abilities, and environmental considerations. At the same time, much more attention is finally being paid to men's parenting abilities, responsibilities, and opportunities for nurture: we now have evidence that fathers "do make good mothers."[45]

Other Routes to Happiness?

Everyone's path to happiness is different.[46]

---

41. Gibb, *Childless Voices*, 4.

42. Gillis, *World of Their Own Making*, 158.

43. Gillis, *World of Their Own Making*, 155.

44. Gillis, *World of Their Own Making*, 178.

45. Boesveld, "Do Fathers Make Good Mothers?"

46. "10 Keys to Happier Living," para. 1.

But what about other paths to happiness—ones that are not intrinsically linked to finding the love of one's life or raising a family? Other alternatives are becoming more prominent, and preoccupation with coupled love or parenting has an increasing number of rivals these days: it would suffice to browse the "Self-help" section of a bookstore, or type in "happiness" into a search browser. Other, or at least additional, variants of a satisfying, happy life are being increasingly suggested, from academic books to glossy magazines and TV programs. Although they may still be perceived as complementary or alternatives in relation to romantic coupling, which is seen as *the* most important thing, they come with a growing recognition that there *are*, indeed, other possibilities.

Much of the bourgeoning happiness industry is related, directly or not, to a specific turn in the field of psychology, commonly known as positive psychology: an interest in what contributes to healthy and positive expressions of life, rather than the anomalous and pathological. Its very appearance a couple of decades ago is indicative of the changes which our societies have been undergoing. Positive psychology has greatly contributed to an understanding, and indeed insistence, that there exist different ways to be happy, and that an individual should be free to choose from among these ways. The title of the popular book by Martin E. P. Seligman captures it well: *Authentic Happiness: Using the New Positive Psychology to Realize Your Potential for Lasting Fulfillment.* The idea gets repeated endlessly in popular culture.

Unsurprisingly, in individualistic societies the spotlight turns onto one's self and personal development: from joining a local book club, to the whole health or beauty or diet industry, to career ambitions. One's personal development can be seen as very "spiritual" or very "down to earth." The more "spiritual" ambitions tend to relate to goals such as becoming more at peace with oneself and the world. Richard Layard writes: "Through education and practice, it is possible to improve your inner life—to accept yourself better and to feel more for others. In most of us there is a deep positive force, which can be liberated if we can overcome our negative thoughts."[47] However, "working on oneself" can also be about perfecting one's body, and gaining, or at least coming closer to, the "right" body image. Rather poignantly, it can also be implicitly linked to finding happiness in love: once one's body is more attractive, one can hope to "catch" a partner.

Still with the focus on one's own person, economic and physical wellbeing also get attention as conditions for happiness.[48] Over the last few decades,

---

47. Layard, *Happiness*, loc. 3405.

48. A commonly suggested triad of happiness or "satisfaction domains" is marriage, economic wellbeing, and health. E.g., Plagnol, "Subjective Well-being," 753.

however, there has been a growing recognition of the need to look beyond oneself. Wider relationships and helping others are increasingly recognized as significantly boosting one's wellbeing, as is participating in causes larger than one's personal life, be they religious affiliation or social activism.[49] It may also be about discovering the world by traveling, being financially independent and therefore gaining the freedom of one's time, or pursuing a meaningful career or creative projects. All these routes to good life are getting increasing exposure in happiness studies as well as in popular culture.

Yet rarely is there a discussion about the criteria of choosing these ways except the need to find the ones that are "authentic" and "will work for you." In other words, the question, "What makes you happy?" is left to be answered by each one of us individually. And here we observe that in spite of all the possible and exciting options, nothing seems to be as pervasive as a combination of romantic love and "having a family," with a bit of personal growth on the side.[50]

Why is that so? One answer, of course, is that this is simply how things are; that happiness, to a great extent, truly lies in the nuclear family and the experience of falling in love, coming together, and raising a family. Yet, as this chapter suggests, our desires and perceptions of happiness are shaped by what we have been taught to aspire for, and here the narrative of a romance with a happy ending (and a happy family) still runs supreme more often than not.

Our desires—our feelings about what would make us happy—do not arise in a vacuum. Much of their shaping happens on the subconscious level, through the pictures and stories we internalize as we grow up and mature. Theologian James K. A. Smith writes: "We are oriented by our longings, directed by our desires. We adopt ways of life that are indexed to such visions of the good life, not usually because we "think through" our options but rather because some picture captures our imagination."[51] Thus, no matter how many times we may be encouraged to search for that "authentic happiness" that would be truly best for us, our vision of a good life will be primarily shaped by what is valued by other people around us. That is also true for those who call themselves Christians.

---

49. For an example representing one of the many initiatives for helping people to cultivate happiness, see ten "keys" to happiness developed by "Action for Happiness." "10 Keys for Happier Living."

50. See, e.g., Kotter-Grühn et al., "What Is It We Are Longing For," 433.

51. Smith, *You Are What You Love*, 11.

Cultural Reflections: Happiness in Christianeze

> Too many single people feel that God's love for them is contingent
> on the presence of a boyfriend or girlfriend, a husband or a wife.
> Too many singles feel that if God really cared for them they would
> still have a spouse. Too many singles wallow in the loneliness that
> can accompany singleness and assume that God is not with them.[52]

If "happiness" is a complicated concept, it is even more so in the Christian
context, where it is often present within the language of following God's will
and being a recipient of God's blessing. It may be expressed as a condition: "if
you obey God's will, then God will grant you happiness." Or, happiness may
be seen as an expression of God's blessing: "God blessed me with . . ." Either
way, this is the question at the heart of the matter: what kind of life can be
considered to be truly good, or what kind of things and circumstances we
should desire?

In this book, I have sought to show that our current desires and our ideas
about happiness are clearly aligned not so much with the vision of a good life
in the New Testament, but with the culture we currently inhabit. What Ronald
Rolheiser observed about American Christian culture is true throughout the
West: "No possibility of real happiness is seen outside [marriage]."[53] Of course,
it does not need to be said explicitly. Here is an observation of a single Christian woman: "In retrospect, it's not that anyone overtly declared to me there
was no joy to be had as a single, celibate woman. It's just that like many of us, I
secretly believed that the *deepest drafts* are to be drunk only by those invited to
a joy party. And the only people invited to that party are those walking in the
marriage/sex/kids shoes. Too bad for me or anyone else stuck wearing these
unsought single shoes."[54]

Unsurprisingly, then, for many, marriage symbolizes the ultimate expression of God's blessing. For those who are single but have come to believe
the link between marriage and God's blessing or God's favor, their singleness
can become a source of deep spiritual anguish too: Have I done something
wrong? Is God punishing me? Why is God not listening to my prayers? Others
give up on their questions and their commitment to the Christian way—or at
least the church which clearly views their lives as less esteemed.

The link between marriage and God's blessing also represents another
picture of happiness not readily available for many single Christians: the

---

52. Patterson, "Singles and the Church," 54.

53. Rolheiser, *Forgotten Among the Lilies*, 51.

54. Gilliam, *Revelations of a Single Woman*, 137. Emphasis in the original.

experience of parenthood. This can be particularly difficult for women approaching the end of their fertile years who belong to communities of faith which do not approve of single motherhood, unless one has become a single mother before becoming a Christian. Yet they may get some understanding of their longings, even in the case of a "slip up": "If I did have a child out of wedlock, it wouldn't have been from a lack of desire to do it the Proper Way, and I suspect some people might even sigh with relief, wondering why I'd never married and glad to know I was Normal after all."[55] These are really powerful streams and undercurrents of perceived happiness to swim against.

How on earth do we get from here to the vision of the good life offered by Jesus to his disciples? It is likely that many local churches, perceiving themselves to be the bastions of Christian truth (or, more precisely, Christendom's truth), will continue treating singleness as a threat against Christian presence and witness. But it is also likely that the cultural stirrings against the domination of marriage and family will turn out to have given the church a precious gift, compelling many Christian communities to re-examine the role of blood and marriage ties within the larger family of God. These communities will need to do some serious work in re-learning happiness, and this is what the last chapter will be about.

---

55. Keay, *Letters from a Solo Survivor*, 66–67.

8

Re-learning Love and Happiness

Singleness and Marriage after Christendom

"Happiness in Relationships":
Glimpses and Dreams of the Church as the Primary Family

> Marriage is subservient to discipleship. Our marriages are ulti-
> mately significant only as a means of supporting each of us in our
> ministry, including the ministries of childrearing, conversion of
> the young, protection of the old.[1]

We have already seen that relationships are commonly recognized as a
key element in sustaining human happiness. Although until recently
marital bonds or blood relations have been the center of attention, there is
a growing recognition that wider links often covered under the headings of
"friendships" and "community" are just as essential to our wellbeing. Moreover,
various other assumptions are also being increasingly challenged. It turns out,
for example, that single people—particularly always-single people—may enjoy better social connections and "are more likely to frequently stay in touch
with, provide help to, and receive help from parents, siblings, neighbors, and
friends than the married."[2] We do not often think of marriage as increasing
our social isolation, but such facts give some food for thought.

---

1. Hauerwas and Willimon, *Where Resident Aliens Live*, 86.
2. Sarkisian and Gerstel, "Does Singlehood Isolate or Integrate," 361.

Let me illustrate this with a real-life story. A woman—single and well-embedded in her community of faith—ends up in a hospital for a semi-serious surgery. News is shared, prayers are offered, and many well-wishing friends want to know how she is doing and whether she needs any help. She receives calls and messages, flowers, get-well cards, and personal visits with practical items or little gifts to cheer her up. Her visitors coordinate their support among themselves, and make sure she is well looked after once she can leave the hospital and recuperate at home. Visits continue as long as she needs support with various daily tasks.

Now imagine the same woman, in a hospital room again, but by now she is married to a loving husband. Just like before, people from her community circle want to know how she is doing, and whether she needs any help. What is the way they choose to find out this information? Mostly, through her husband: it seems natural for everybody to call him, or perhaps he insists that visits be coordinated through him. Flowers may be sent, as will be cards with get well wishes, but for most of her time in hospital, the only, or at least the primary, visitor this woman will receive is her husband, who will pass on the news and the gifts and anything else she may have asked him to bring.

Of course, this is not a universal example. Many single people would say they lack a social network of deep, meaningful relationships—but then, if pressed, so would a number of people in their marriages. One's gender, age, and particular culture will also play a role. Yet as a whole, the singles who feel well-integrated into their communal network often live much richer social lives compared to those who are married. In that sense, the contemporary Western version of marriage often turns out to be, as some researchers put it, a "greedy institution": it "weakens both women's and men's ties to those other than the spouse."[3]

For today's faith communities which so often associate church with nuclear families, this is a much-needed reminder of how much the church actually *needs* single people: they will often be a significant prophetic voice calling to a life beyond our own home and comfort zone. Just as in the early Christian experience, though for different reasons, singles today can offer an eschatological reminder, pointing to the kingdom of God and the fullness of life that can already be tasted in the here and now. As we seek that kingdom, we also discover a new family—God's family—which becomes an integral part of our life and learning to follow the Way of Jesus.

And yet as I write this, I am painfully aware of how far the reality of today's average church may be from such a picture. For the majority, the church

3. Sarkisian and Gerstel, "Marriage," 19. For the origin of the phrase "greedy institution," see Coser and Coser, "Stay Home."

is not really the primary family in any tangible way. For some, it is on the level of a Sunday club: a sufficiently pleasant and respectable weekly activity. For others, it is an expression of the longing for more and deeper connections with those we refer to as "sisters and brothers in Christ." Yet such deeper connections seem to be precluded by the shape of daily living: geographical distance between church members, overflowing daily schedules, and so on. Even making it to the church meeting regularly can be difficult given the juggling of work and various home responsibilities.

Finding some kind of a genuine community-shaped life that embodies our faith is one of the most difficult challenges we face in today's fragmented, time-poor, deeply consumerist Western context. Various community expressions are sought and tried: from traditional monasteries to "new monasticism"; from churches which commit to living in close geographical proximity, often intentionally in a poor neighborhood, to networks of dispersed or online communities. The recent experience of the global pandemic, when churches in many parts of the world had to move online, opened up new ways of thinking about church forms, while also highlighting the importance of face-to-face connections. New shapes and expressions of Jesus' Way will hopefully continue emerging; perhaps some of the readers of this book will feel a stir to be a catalyst for one of them.

At the same time, the frustration with the current shape of the church has led others to groups only loosely associated with organized Christianity, but which they deem as being closer to Jesus' vision of a faith-full life. People joining these communities will often have been burned by their experience of the traditional church, so thin on community and so wedded to the assumptions of Christendom, and they find solace in organic intentional communities where people take seriously an invitation to do life together as they seek justice and peace in the name of Jesus.

Whatever the form, fostering "happy" single lives and "happy" marriages in the Christian context will be directly related to the presence of genuine communities of faith—a topic explored in several other books in the *After Christendom* series.[4] In the volume which started the series, Stuart Murray noted the importance of such characteristics as shared meals, an ability to laugh together, and becoming friends as the basic elements of sustaining church as community after Christendom.[5] Among these features, friendship has a particular significance for rethinking happiness in relation to singleness and marriage. And so we turn next to consider some key shared experiences of Christian life, including the practice of friendship.

4. E.g., Francis, *Hospitality and Community*.
5. Murray, *Post-Christendom*, 202.

Happiness Revised:
Perceptions, Words, Actions, and Practices

> Happiness is understood as a particular kind of human response to the way things are which, however apparently spontaneous in expression, is learned within a context of community, tradition, moral norms, and family life. Happiness, we may say, arises out of a deep, culturally-mediated sense of alignment with reality, with life in families playing a key role.[6]

How can the communities of Jesus' disciples swim against the stream of our love-and-coupledom fixated understanding of what constitutes a fulfilled and happy life? It is certainly going to be a long-term project, given how deeply ingrained our present ideas of a good life are. For the same reason, it will have to be tackled through various means and in different areas of communal and personal life.

A reconsideration of happiness can start with new ways of engaging with the Scripture and the scandalously radical message of Jesus. Stephen Barton suggests that we keep returning to Jesus' question, "Who are my mother and my brothers?" As we have seen in the previous chapters, modernity has convinced us "to make the family—the nuclear family, in particular—the *sole measure* of human relationships in general."[7] For our times, therefore, Jesus' question is a powerful reminder "that the family is *not an end in itself* and that modernity's 'idolatry of the family' stands under judgement. It says to us that belonging to Jesus and the 'new' family of Jesus—theologically speaking, the church—is the prior, more profound (because eschatological) reality to which human beings are called."[8]

However, Jesus' question, for Barton, also carries a challenging message for our increasingly postmodern context in which personal identity becomes an ever greater struggle; an age that is "plural, plastic and negotiable in ways previously unknown."[9] For people who are faced with an array of identity narratives to choose from, the message offered by the church of Jesus is an invitation to a place of belonging and identity which transcends our personal struggles and contradictions, but also welcomes us as we are—with all those struggles and contradictions—so that we can begin making sense of them in the light of the calling into the life of the kingdom.

---

6. Barton, "Finding Happiness," 6.

7. Barton, *Life Together*, 47. Emphasis in the original.

8. Barton, *Life Together*, 48. Emphasis in the original.

9. Barton, *Life Together*, 49.

Such a reordered worldview, therefore, provides a different context for the life of marriage and family—a context without which the weight of meaning-making often becomes too heavy for marriages and families to shoulder. And while it may be perceived as an attack against marriage and the nuclear family, in fact they are strengthened by this broader framework: freed from the impossible obligation of self-sufficiency, couples and families can be sustained by the larger rhythms of community life and its mission.

Yet another area from which to start reconsidering our culturally conditioned views of a fulfilling life is the idea of choices and decisions, and especially the burden of such (made, of course, "individually" and "responsibly"). We often think of this as a particular predicament for single people especially: "Have I been too picky? Or do I possess the 'gift' of singleness and therefore am I called to a life of singleness?" However, this may be an even more daunting reality for the married ones, many of whom at one time or another have been quietly questioning their "decision" to marry their spouse. Often endured in silence, the possibility of a "wrong decision" can cause terrible anguish. How freeing, then, can re-envisioning our vocation (or the will of God, or discovering our passion or purpose) be when it releases us from such weight of our own past decisions. Indeed, "the most reliable callings are born from reflecting on a situation that is more or less imposed on us. A vocation is nearly always a way of accepting a situation that was first of all considered a limitation."[10]

Perceptions of happiness can also be confronted and transformed by the revision of the way we talk about the shape of our lives. This includes both formal language (e.g., the service of worship, including the sermon) and informal (e.g., chats after the service over coffee and personal communication). Both, I suggest, are equally important and equally formative.

Preaching and teaching are obvious opportunities to revisit Jesus' message and discover how it reshapes our understanding of marriage and family. Using examples—from Scripture and contemporary life—that do not assume marriage as the norm would be a significant step. Hopefully chapters 2 and 3 of this book can be of help for those involved in such ministries, and opening up to all that fascinatingly unsettling world of the Bible. And then there is so much work in addressing the varieties of contemporary contexts in our sermons, Bible studies, and various other teaching and learning opportunities: recognizing different family shapes; calling all, whether married or single, into a life of hospitality; and helping us to make sense of our own questions and potential trajectories of life.

---

10. Mehl, *Society and Love*, quoted in Clapp, *Families at the Crossroads*, 89.

However, equal attention should be paid to more informal communication, including well-meant advice or comments on the lives of others. These will reflect our actual theology—our worldview—most accurately. Some changes are obvious and relatively easy: referring to someone's spouse as their "other half" is common, but given the myth of humans destined to search for their "missing half" (see chapter 6) it implies that single people simply cannot be ever complete on their own. Some other linguistic revisions will be more challenging and require a good deal of creativity as well as determination. Here a lot will depend on a particular language. As noted in the Introduction to this volume, in some languages "singleness" and "loneliness," or "alone" and "lonely" are covered by the same word. In such cases actively searching for words and phrases for singleness that do not assume loneliness is likely to be lengthy and awkward, yet, I would argue, a necessary process. We can, however, draw some inspiration from efforts to get away from equating God with maleness in our speaking of God—a tricky task for heavily gendered languages especially, but we already know that progress can be made and things can change. A regular "language audit" might be a particularly helpful ministry for a community of faith, as long as it does not function as a "language police" but is offered and received with sensitivity and desire to reflect the values of the kingdom which Jesus preached.

Just as our language shapes our worldview, so do our actions and practices—those we intentionally choose to take part in as well as those we embrace without much reflection. An inclusive community will seek to welcome the gifts that each person brings to the church. In this, single people who are exercising leadership roles in the community will be challenging an implicit and deeply harmful belief that singleness is somehow related to immaturity and the lack of experience.

In the context of meeting as a church, we would do well to pay attention to the way we tend to "cluster," and where possible arrange spaces and activities in such a way that encourages couples to disperse and enjoy meeting people they would not naturally run into in their own circles, and those who come on their own would have a chance to get to know others as persons, not only as couples. Such "mixing" is likely to be welcomed by the singles, but it would also enrich and support marriages through their different stages and situations, expanding the horizons of the relationships that can become locked in their own, coupled, isolation. It will also be vital for those who are "single as Christians"—that is, they are married, but their spouse does not take part in the community of faith, so they are, in fact, on their own any time they are in the church.

Another area for some further thought is an expansion of rites of passage that can be celebrated in the church. In the observation of one single person, "the problem is not the way in which those rituals are celebrated, but the fact that those rituals do not have a counterbalance of rituals that celebrate things in the life of a single person that are of equal importance."[11] If marriage, or renewal of the marriage vows, and marriage anniversaries are to be part of the community's common joy, what milestones of single life can we celebrate together too? Furthermore, what rites and rituals, private or public, could help with the grief that often accompanies a disintegration of a relationship? Asking such questions, or creating space for writing such materials, will not only encourage and support people who have so far been excluded from such meaning-making markers of their lives, but will also create an environment for careful and sensitive listening to each others' life stories, and therefore a deepening sense of a community that truly does life together.[12]

These are just some examples which may be used as a starting point for reflection and conversation. Of course, they will differ depending on the community's size, cultural factors, and the particular places or formats of gathering together. But hopefully they may provide some inspiration for asking questions about the way we think, talk, act, and take part in different practices. They also point to the fact that our participation in the community of faith should be our place of formation—the school in which we learn how to live our lives. To highlight one instance of such formation, let us briefly look at one particular practice: friendship.

Becoming Friends: An Invitation to a Re-envisioned Personal, Communal, and Missional Practice

> The pleasure of good food and conversation with people one enjoys and trusts is symbolic of fulfilment at a very deep level. . . . Sharing of food, like friendship itself, is potentially a more inclusive phenomenon than sex.[13]

Friendship is important not only for our personal wellbeing, but also for the common life of the body of Christ, which is further extended in befriending those outside the church, in the manner of the One who was accused of being

---

11. An interviewee's response, Clapp, *Families at the Crossroads*, 218.

12. For an example of a collection of worship resources which takes different life changes seriously, see Ward and Wild, *Human Rites*.

13. McFague, *Models of God*, 167.

a "friend of sinners." As I have argued elsewhere, all three modes of friend-ship—personal, communal, and missional—are just as important.[14] They are also interconnected: that is, our openness to another human being and the vulnerability that it requires expressed in personal, intimate friendships shapes the way we extend friendship to those with whom we would naturally never associate, save that somehow we have been brought together through the work of Christ.

What happens in the church (or an intentional Christian community, or an informal group of Jesus' disciples by some other name) is going to be im-mensely formative for the way we practice both our personal friendships and our befriending of those to whom we extend our friendship in the name of Jesus. As Paul Wadell suggests, the church is to be "a befriending community that not only welcomes all who come to it but also offers them a place where the grammar of intimacy and friendship can be learned."[15] In this school of friendship, we can learn what it means to live hospitably—a life-long lesson that is essential for any household that imagines itself to be Christian. Such hospitable friendship invites us to step outside our comfort zones and extend our homes, hearts, and time to all kinds of different people.

Lest we think this is something we do for others (or perhaps even "for God"), it is likely to turn out to be a great enrichment, or even transformation, of our own lives. Dinners together, or walks in the park, or joint activities such as cleaning up a local area can be one of the most effective ways of addressing the lack of depth in our church experience. While "church" gatherings might still happen only on a weekly basis, homes (and cafes, and places we volunteer together, and so on) can be the places where we get to know others and let ourselves be known. In such deeper knowing, both marriage and singleness can be supported, lived out, and seen by others in a realistic light.

Some of such friendships may well grow into a more stable form of intentional community life, including shared homes. Creating new kinds of households can take many forms; the Beguine experience highlighted in chap-ter 5 can serve as one of the inspirations.[16] Although many recent experiments have not been greatly successful,[17] intentional communal living continues to captivate the minds of many of those who are thinking about the practice of faith after Christendom. Those who have been privileged to experience life in a healthy intentional community know how much it resonates with the vision of Jesus for those whom he called his friends. Which is not to say that it is an

14. Toth, "Befriending."
15. Wadell, *Becoming Friends*, 53.
16. E.g., Howard, "Beguine Option."
17. E.g., Christian, *Creating Life Together*.

easy option: intentional community life can be really hard at times, especially if it has been entered into without a good dose of realism and understanding of people's varying long-term needs. Yet such creative households are an under-used resource for re-learning happiness in a world of housing issues, economic shortages, and a pervading experience of loneliness and isolation.

. . . But What About Sex?
Happiness and Redefinitions of the Body

> If human sexuality has to do with how we communicate desire
> for 'the other' through our bodiliness . . . it is important that we
> understand this kind of communication as much as possible.[18]

Some readers may have found the discussion so far frustrating: why have sexuality and sexual relationships not been more at the center? Isn't that a crucial area of human experience to address? Moreover, doesn't the church have a lot to answer for long centuries of disparaging sex, equating it with sin, and attempting to control people's sexual lives? Surely an acknowledgement of the central role that sex plays in human lives is a welcome and necessary corrective?

Today's Western world subscribes to the idea that no one is really living life to its fullness unless they have a sexual outlet: "Good sex is an inseparable part of our well-being and happiness."[19] Or, in the Christianized version, "God, don't let me die before I can have sex!"[20] Yet what does such deeply held conviction mean in those churches which insist that single Christians should remain celibate, because sex ought to be reserved for marriage? The answer comes by the way of statistics: in the US context, even though a great majority of evangelicals would support "sex only in marriage" position, "eighty percent of young, unmarried Christians have had sex. Two-thirds have been sexually active in the last year."[21] Or here is a quote from a survey among British Christians: "I definitely think [sex] is supposed to be in the context of a loving committed relationship. But I also find it hard to believe that as sexual beings it would be God's plan that I'm still a virgin if I'm single at 65."[22] There is a lot of

18. Barton, *Life Together*, 73.

19. Assari, "Consensual Sex," para. 3.

20. As expressed by several interviewees in *Give Me Sex Jesus*—a documentary on the evangelical purity culture.

21. Charles, "Secret Sexual Revolution," 66.

22. "What Do Christians Think," para. 39.

frustration, also, for single believers who are expected to focus on their sexual purity, without any further help or guidance beyond "don't!" As one woman put it, "Christian leaders assume that our sexuality is like a faucet that you only turn on when you get married."[23] Not surprisingly, acknowledging the reality on the ground, a growing number of churches are turning a blind eye to the private lives of their single members, and other churches and church leaders are openly offering a different kind of Christian view on human sexuality.[24]

What, then, do we do about sex and happiness? By not addressing the issue until now I am making a point: whenever sexual activity becomes the focus, we will inescapably fall into one of a few traps. On the one hand, we may consider the power of the sexual urges as inescapable and irresistible. What can one do but capitulate (or marry as soon as possible)—unless, that is, one has that mysterious "gift of singleness" which would automatically solve the problem? Of course, that creates a particular anguish for those who are single and celibate yet wishing they were married, but it also can complicate married life: what to do if marital sex turns out to be less than wonderful and less than plentiful?

The other trap represents the opposite end of the same assumption: if sexual urge is so powerful, it is to be feared and is too dangerous to be ever genuinely enjoyed. And because our bodily urges are never to be trusted, our relationships with others are to be strictly regulated, even if that means forgoing most, or all of, bodily contact with other human beings. As we have seen, this has been tried time and again throughout Christian history. Human bodies come to be seen as vessels that can be "broken" by any sexual activity that is not marital. Such a purity paradigm easily leads to a very harmful commodification of the body (especially the female body), as recently acknowledged by some of the previous proponents of contemporary Christian purity culture. Reflecting on how his thinking has changed since his bestselling *I Kissed Dating Goodbye*, Joshua Harris now admits: "The book . . . gave some the impression that a certain methodology of relationships [such as no dating and no kissing before marriage] would deliver a happy ever-after ending—a great marriage, a great sex life—even though this is not promised by scripture. To those who read my book and were misdirected or unhelpfully influenced by it, I am sincerely sorry."[25] The survivors of sexual abuse also witness the impact of the focus on sexual purity in the wake of their trauma: "I felt like

---

23. Gaddini, "Why Are So Many Single Women Leaving the Church?," para. 12.

24. E.g., Bolz-Weber, "Denver Statement."

25. Harris, "Statement," para. 6.

I wasn't even human anymore. . . . You no longer have worth, you no longer have value."[26]

In the light of these two traps, then, what can be said about the relationship between happiness and sex? A common place to start is the wider context: "sexuality" rather than simply "sex." Sexuality, or our erotic capacity, can be understood as an invitation to a deeper experience and delight in God, other humans, and God's created world. We could also say that sexuality is about our connectedness as human beings. Here is one way to describe it: "Sexuality is the drive in us toward connection, community, family, friendship, affection, love, creativity, and generativity. We are happy and whole when these things are in our lives, not on the basis of whether or not we sleep alone."[27] Indeed, this can be a helpful way to think about our response to beauty, intellectual stimulation, or various kinds of human connections we experience during our lives.

But what does "sexuality" say to someone struggling with their own sexual identity? What does it mean for someone who is asexual or physically unable to have sexual intercourse? How would it sound to someone who, due to the drop of hormonal levels, feels their erotic desires have receded? How does it really help a gay person who, alongside their community of faith, believes that gay people should remain celibate? Of course, the larger framework of sexuality as human connection and experience of delight still applies, but I wonder if it is really that helpful as a category for our purposes here. Furthermore, in the post-Eden world, sexuality always carries within itself some dark shadows, for people both in and without sexual relationships: it is always "broken," in more ways than one, and therefore in a desperate need of a larger framework within which to make sense of its urges.[28]

How, then, about attending to an even broader context in which we function: our life as bodies? Regardless of how we understand or experience gender, sex, or sexuality, one thing really unites all living human beings, and that is our bodiliness. It is as embodied beings that we experience life and all our relationships with others. Whatever our bodies are at the moment—relatively healthy or not, old or young, female or male, sexually active or not—it is through them that we sense our satisfaction with life or the lack thereof.

Once we start with the reality of our bodies, we may be less tempted to reduce the complexity of the human need for intimacy to the need for sexual intercourse. Instead, we can begin offering appropriate encouragement and

26. Elizabeth Smart, a survivor of kidnap and long-term rape, in Hall, "Elizabeth Smart," paras. 3, 10.

27. Rolheiser, *Forgotten Among the Lilies*, 52.

28. Gushee, *Changing Our Mind*, 97.

support, emotional and physical, that each human being needs, including those who are single. Once such human needs are not negated and not ascribed to the sexual drive only, there will be something for all of us to learn: how to love, comfort, affirm, and appreciate each other, including those who do not have the exclusive rights to the intimacy of one person.

A further exploration may lead to asking questions about the commonly held (though not necessarily biblical) separation of the human being into a body and a soul (or, in another variation, also a spirit). Some recent conversations with biblical scholars and neuroscientists suggest that it would be much more fruitful to think of a human being holistically. In such a view, "our 'soulishness' should be understood as our relatedness to God, to other humans, and to all of creation. . . . I do not have a soul, I *am* a living being, or soul."[29]

This is particularly important in light of the general disregard, disdain, and distrust for the body that has accompanied Christian theology for centuries: there is clearly a lot of work to be done to bring back the human body into the experience of faith and Christian community life. However, there have been some fascinating exceptions in centuries past, too. In chapter 5, we briefly looked at the way medieval monastics wrestled with their own bodies—at times mortifying the flesh in the attempt to stop the bodily urges, but at other times treating the body as the place where God is experienced. The sense of *bodily* devotion, all our five senses actively participating in worship, has a lot to say to our present struggles.

Perhaps it is not too surprising that recent years have seen a renewed interest in asceticism and monasticism—yet notably, not so much in the church as in popular culture and in academia. "'Ascetic rigour' can in some circumstances not only 'sublimate' sexual desire but itself represent an enticing (even 'sexy'!) alternative, one that precisely attracts the attention of the postmodern scholar of late antiquity for its zaniness, its resistance of normalcy, its power to change the 'rules' of society."[30] Sarah Coakley, the theologian I quote here, draws attention to trends in sport or the diet industry which echo the same ages-old ascetic obsession with "personal 'control' over resistant 'flesh.'"[31] As a response to a highly sexualized culture, some are discovering the freedom which self-imposed celibacy brings: it can feel like a "massive relief. I stopped seeing men as sex objects and females as competition."[32] In the United States,

---

29. Jeeves, "Nature of Persons," 71. For a further discussion of non-reductive view of the body and sexuality, see Andronovienė, *Transforming the Struggles*, 186–99.

30. Coakley, *New Asceticism*, 22.

31. Coakley, *New Asceticism*, 21.

32. Eleanor Conway, a British comedian. In Cernik, "Power of Celibacy," para. 2.

the current proportion of people staying celibate is higher than ever before, largely due to rapidly growing number of young people—particularly men—reporting that they are not sexually active.[33] Some of these are not celibate by choice, as illustrated by the deeply disturbing, extremist movement of incels, or "involuntary celibates."[34] Yet the vast majority of today's secular celibates serves as a reminder that, contrary to what one might conclude from the mainstream culture, the absence of sexual outlet may not be such a big deal for basic human happiness.

And, of course, celibacy is not limited to being single. Some couples opt for a celibate relationship simply because sex does not matter much to either of the partners: "We . . . both agree that we have enhanced each other's lives so much. Sex just isn't that important to everyone."[35] Many other couples will experience short or prolonged periods of sexual abstinence because of health, children, or relationship dynamics. Indeed, as Coakley points out, we need to challenge the "assumption that celibacy and marriage are somehow *opposites*, with one ostensibly involving no 'sex' at all, and the other, again supposedly, involving as much sex as one or both partners might like at any one time."[36] She continues:

> A *realistic* reflection on long and faithful marriages . . . will surely reveal periods of enforced "celibacy" even *within* marriages. . . . The reflective, faithful celibate and the reflective, faithful married person may have more in common—by way of prayerful surrendering of inevitably *thwarted* desire to God—than the unreflective or faithless celibate, or the carelessly happy, or indeed unhappily careless, married person.[37]

What we have here, then, is an invitation to avoid both traps which arise out of giving sex more attention and power than is right: neither denying the force of erotic urges, nor treating them as if they were everything, and as if we were utterly helpless in their wake. At least this is where we should start. Once we stop lumping marriage with sex, and singleness with celibacy, some deeper and more helpful questions can be asked about bodily happiness, and indeed bodily spirituality. The rest will have to be worked out in our particular communities of faith as they wrestle with our own (at times contradictory) cultural norms, grapple with how these norms square with the spirit of the

33. Ingraham, "Share of Americans."
34. Williams, "Raw Hatred."
35. Cernik, "Power of Celibacy," para. 11.
36. Coakley, *New Asceticism*, 38.
37. Coakley, *New Asceticism*, 38–39. Emphasis in the original.

kingdom of God they discover in Scriptures, and support both singles and couples trying to make sense of their own bodily needs and desires.

In the beginning of this section, I observed that some readers may feel frustration about how late the discussion on sexuality has come. I suspect there may be even more frustration at this point, given all that has still not been said. What, for example, of same-sex relationships and same-sex marriage? Or what about "guidelines" for unmarried Christians who are dating?

These are certainly important questions, but this book would not be able to do justice to them: they require a focus of their own. Fortunately, resources are being produced to help Christian communities make sense of these, and related, issues that have become a symbol of the major societal changes with which today's churches grapple.[38] What is clear, however, is that the starting point for the church after Christendom is to delve deeper than the questions of "allowed" or "forbidden." For those who truly search for the guidance of the Spirit in today's world, there will be no option but to engage with Scripture, expecting it to shed light on the situations and the information we have today. Various interpretations of biblical texts and their history will be important to understand in terms of the churches' changing role in society. But also, as I propose above, there will be important work to be done around reimagining the body's engagement in communal worship and fostering a healthy perspective toward the look of individual bodies within the community. And while what we do in private has a bearing on the corporate adventure of the community of Jesus, there is also space for the mystery of our functioning as bodies, "fearfully and wonderfully made" (Ps 139:14). If we are able to hold this tension, we may be in a better place to address the particular challenges we face today in the area of human sexuality and life lived to its fullness.

Fertile Happiness: Creativity, Suffering, and Meaning-Making

> The person who loves life in the light of the resurrection hope becomes capable of happiness. All the senses come awake, the understanding and the heart become open for the beauty of this life. But with this love for life we also become capable of suffering, and feel the pains, the disappointments and the trouble of this mortal life. . . . We experience what life and death really are when we love, for in love we go out of ourselves, become capable of happiness

38. On the issue of same-sex relationships, see, for instance, Gushee, *Changing our Minds*; Keen, *Scripture, Ethics, and the Possibility of Same-Sex Relationships*; and on the argument for celibacy for gay Christians, see Hill, *Washed and Waiting*. For an overview of different thoughtful theological positions on the subject, see Sprinkle, *Two Views*.

and at the same time can be hurt.[39]

As we approach the end of this book, we return to a few of the biblical and historical highlights noted in the earlier chapters. Let us start with this reminder of one of the central features of early Christianity: it was a movement that was to grow not through marriages and the birth of the next generation, but through conversion. The kingdom of God they expected, and in some ways already inhabited, was not based on the link between death and the necessity to reproduce in order for life to continue. At the same time, children were to be loved and protected (rather than left to die or be exploited), and valued not for the potential they represented, but for their intrinsic worth as God's gifts. If this important feature is to find its appropriate expressions today, at the very least, it calls for resisting attitudes which treat children as accessories, warranties, or stamps of approval.

It also means that children (and marriages, and single lives) are to be part of the larger whole, that is, the life of the community of God that longs, hopes for, and works for the coming of the kingdom in its fullness. Here the wisdom of the past we explored earlier brings us back to a broader meaning of parenting which is not limited to biological or nuclear parenting, but offers different ways in which we may be called to be mothers or fathers. It also challenges us to regain the sense of the church community as a family, its children in some ways cared for and nurtured by all, not only biological or adoptive parents.

While the link between fertility and procreation or parenting others in our lives is the most obvious, there are many other ways we can join in the fascinating task of co-creating with God. Indeed, all expressions of human creativity testify to the image of God that each of us bears. As we ourselves are God's "masterpiece," "handiwork" or "accomplishment" (Eph 2:10), our own creativity is expressed in a multitude of ways. It is at the heart of who we are, and how we deal with whatever life throws at us. Although it ought to be an essential aspect of our working life as well as leisure, sadly, this is not many people's experience. Yet those who are fortunate to know the joy of getting lost in some activity they are engaged in—what positive psychology calls "flow"—have grasped a key element of flourishing.[40]

Creativity is also present in the ways we navigate and nurture our relationships with others, especially when we—and those relationships—continue to evolve over the years. If anything, creativity is an essential ingredient in the recipe for sustaining love within marriage that is to last beyond the initial

---

39. Moltmann, *Sun of Righteousness, Arise*, 64.

40. Csikszentmihalyi, *Flow*.

surge of romance. Similarly, it is indispensable if we are to adapt and craft new points of connection with other family members and friends. Furthermore, we need creativity in our communal experience of being a church, especially as we seek to worship God with many incarnations of a "new song" (Ps 98:1). And, whether together with others or alone, creative engagement is central to our enjoyment of beauty and nature as well as to our artistic endeavors; this is as true of those who do not think of themselves at all as "artistic," as it is of lovers of arts or crafts.

Yet, as any artist would confirm, the creative process also involves sweat and tears, at least at times. This does not mean that pain is necessary for humans to be creative, but the experience of an artist's work brings together happiness and suffering, not as opposites, but as a description of our existence. One of the most interesting places to observe this reality is the book of Psalms. So many of the psalms are full of complaint and grieving, but also of the language of happiness and blessedness. Biblical scholar Brent A. Strawn describes this move from lament to praise as the proclamation of the "triumph of life": "a thick description of happiness, one that includes real suffering and a mature view of life that recognizes the existence of true joy and pain."[41]

Such a description would be recognized by many who had to learn deep, authentic happiness amidst adversity and suffering. Married or single life can be the arenas of such suffering too—often for reasons beyond our control; at other times brought about by our own actions. In either case, they can become the places to learn a much deeper—creative—way of being happy, one that involves looking beyond oneself, indeed in a particular way "forgetting oneself," and in that process, discovering oneself anew.

An even more recognizable image, perhaps, is Jesus' description of a grain of wheat that must die for new life to come (John 12:24)—an uncomfortable picture, and one that can also be misused in order to ignore, or even support, just the kind of suffering that we should be working to eradicate. But the depth of this imagery will be familiar to scientists and theologians reflecting on the presence of pain and struggle as part of life: "All living things must participate not only in the taking of life in order to live but also in the painful *giving* of their lives that others might live."[42]

How are we then to live, creatively and happily, with suffering and struggle being part of our existence? Responding to this question will require continuing conversations with other followers of the Way of Jesus. We may

---

41. Strawn, "Triumph of Life," 287.

42. Murphy and Ellis, *On the Moral Nature of the Universe*, 213. Emphasis in the original. I explore this conversation between theology and science in Andronovienė, *Transforming the Struggles*, chapter 9.

also be interested in gleaning some insights from positive psychology and happiness studies, which point to the importance of expanding our focus beyond ourselves in order to flourish, and to the role that adversity can play in some of the most significant personal and communal transformations. Positive psychology's interest in positive institutions as a significant building block for the flourishing of humans is, I think, a challenge to the church, not least in light of some of the recent stories underscoring the oppressive, toxic, life-negating nature of some faith communities. Can the church be such a "positive institution"—indeed, not just an institution, but a social organism, a family system, an intentional community—which brings about and supports a much healthier, broader, deeper understanding and practice of happiness?

In order to affirm the goodness of life as a gift of God, we will need a deeper understanding of the creative process which can transform the experience of going through adversity or pain.[43] In this process, we are invited to make meaning of the different and changing circumstances we may find ourselves in. For the followers of the risen Jesus, such meaning-making is an essential aspect of a happy and fulfilled life. My hope is that the examples and questions with which we have wrestled throughout this book will offer some help and inspiration to those who yearn for such creative meaning-making in their own lives—both as either single or married individuals, and as communities of God's people.

---

43. It was Martin Luther King Jr. who in his "I Have a Dream" speech called those suffering from racist oppression "the veterans of creative suffering." The readers may be interested in three other significant Christian thinkers who have written on the subject of creative suffering: Iulia de Beausobre (*Creative Suffering*), Paul Tournier (*Creative Suffering*), and Paul S. Fiddes (*Creative Suffering of God*).

Conclusion

We will, with the angels, have a life with God and one another where there is no aloneness to be overcome.[1]

In this book, we have been pondering a marked and complex change taking place in the makeup of Western societies. The decline of marriage rates, the ease of divorce, and the decision some couples have taken not to marry at all have all contributed to the sense that the familiar form of marriage and family is dwindling, replaced by much less uniform and much more fluid ways of setting up and negotiating relationships and households. Meanwhile, single people have become the fastest-growing demographic in our societies. It is not difficult to see why the rise of singleness is seen by some as a contributor to the demise of "traditional" marriage and family patterns. As these particular patterns have become so closely associated with the church, their passing is perceived as a threat to its life and identity, especially as the church no longer has control over public issues such as marriage law. More than that, some view the rise of singlehood and the decline of marriage as a threat not only to the survival of the church, but also to that of Western civilization.

The chapters of this book have offered a very different storyline, tracing various outlooks on singleness and marriage in light of the Scripture, Christian tradition, and the history of Christendom. We observed how central marriage and having children were for the people of Israel, and how challenging the words of Jesus must have seemed when he insisted on the husbands' complete faithfulness to their wives, but also celebrated those who chose to forgo marriage for the sake of the kingdom. His vision, seeped in the prophetic tradition, was of a new kind of a family. Those who were drawn to his teaching and believed that God had raised Jesus from the dead after his gruesome death,

1. Hauerwas, *Matthew*, 345.

had to be willing to trust that following Jesus and welcoming the in-breaking kingdom of God was worth the price of reordering all earthly relationships.

Although at times entire households committed to the Way of Jesus, for many others their Christian allegiance meant leaving their previous identity and economic security, and joining an alternative support system—a new-order family called the church. While sometimes the early churches sought to adapt to the societal norms of the time, overall their practices were seen as an affront to existing family patterns. Thus we followed the story of the first centuries of Christianity, when Christians were being accused of destroying the very foundations of a good and orderly society. One of the starkest examples of the Christian clash with the prevailing norms was their embrace of asceticism and celibacy, which went against the imperial policy requiring all Roman citizens to be married. Of course, many Christians still married, but the practice of celibacy embodied the Christian conviction that the kingdom of God was already within reach. As for those who were married, having children was no longer the key element of what it meant to live in God's will, or how faith was to be passed on, or how death was to be overcome.

Much of the subsequent story of marriage and singleness was enmeshed in the long era of Christianization, starting with Emperor Constantine's decisions to embrace Christianity in the fourth century, to the baptism of Lithuania, Europe's last pagan country, in the late fourteenth century. We saw how Christendom's culture picked up the early Christian enthusiasm for celibacy and established it as a superior state to marriage—and considerably holier. Or at least this was the official line: what went on in practice was a different matter, as illustrated by the length of time it took to enforce priestly celibacy in the Western church. Officially, too, marriage was a lifetime event and the only legitimate outlet for sexual relations and procreation; divorce and subsequent remarriage were prohibited. The eventual inclusion of marriage as one of the sacraments of the Catholic Church reflects such an understanding of marriage as an indissoluble bond.

Christendom also encompassed lesser known forms of singlehood and alternative family arrangements—religious revival movements, confraternities, and guilds. In the words of the historian John Gillis, by the late medieval era "these spiritual families were a ubiquitous feature of the European social landscape, assisting at births, celebrating marriages, burying the dead, providing homes away from home on a long- or short-term basis—in other words, offering the kind of services we expect today only from immediate family and close kin."[2] A similar description would have fitted various Anabaptist groupings too. Many of them were ready to pay the ultimate price—that of

2. Gillis, *World of Their Own Making*, 26.

their own lives—as a sign of their commitment to the form of living into which God was calling them. Whether in marriage or singleness, the new and true family of God was a clear center of their life and faith.

During the period of the Reformation, the abuses of enforced celibacy became one of the focal points in the preaching of the Protestant reformers. Before too long, the newly Protestant lands were marked by a culture of suspicion towards those who were single without a "good" reason. But in contrast to the medieval Roman Catholic position which saw marriage's primary purpose in procreation, the magisterial Reformation brought to the fore the idea of companionate marriage and the value of emotional bonds between husband and wife.

In the wake of the Industrial Revolution, marriage became increasingly understood in romantic and emotional terms, with the family home functioning as a sphere of moral purity, secluded from a bustling world. As this new Victorian ideal took root, it also came to represent the pinnacle of human happiness that could be achieved here on earth. This is the worldview we have inherited, and under the power of which we largely still live: we are expected to "marry in the name of passionate love, which should, by and large, then last forever."[3] The contemporary wedding industry is an illustration of romance's continuing enthrallment, and an indication of how much power it still wields even in the face of widespread cohabitation and divorce.

As romance and coupledom became the embodiment of the Western idea of personal happiness, singleness became associated with unfulfilled hopes or an inherently inferior kind of life. The persistence of these associations has been remarkable. Even though the currently burgeoning happiness industry keeps affirming and encouraging an exploration of different pathways to happiness, and singles and single households continue to grow in numbers, the sense of marriage and coupledom as a norm prevails, even if serially. The same can be said of the church: while it is acknowledged that God's will may lead us to a path which does not involve marriage, romantic love and becoming a happy couple still function as the ultimate sign and symbol of God's blessing. Such *de facto* theology stands in stark contrast with the worldview we saw portrayed in the New Testament.

As we watch Christendom melting away, how can our single lives and marriages, and our perceptions of a good life, become aligned with the teaching of Jesus? We have looked at some key areas of life which may help us in this process of conversion. We have considered the theology of singleness and marriage that is, or should be, reflected in our formal and informal communication. We explored the importance of friendship, understood not only

3. Dolan, *Happy Ever After*, 66.

in personal and intimate terms, but also as a community-building and missional practice to which we are invited as the *friends of Jesus*. However, such a practice of friendship needs a genuine community of belonging—a safe and transformative environment for making sense of our bodily yearnings and the difficult, at times painful, twists and turns of our lives. There, with other friends of Jesus, we can make meaning of our own lives in their different seasons, and learn a much deeper and broader sense of fertility and creativity.

That is the trajectory offered in the preceding pages. Of course, there are also many things not covered, and some important questions have remained at the periphery. For example, one obvious issue is that of divorce. The words of Jesus on divorce are painful to hear for many who have lived through the disintegration of a long-term relationship. We did observe, however, that Jesus spoke into a culture in which the husband had all the power to instigate the divorce, and the wife had none. We may also note how harmful the insistence of preserving an abusive marriage can be, and ask whether some marriages die years prior to the divorce. However, the fact remains that many Christian marriages do not survive, and that it is yet another sign of brokenness in the body of Christ. No divorce should be taken lightly, but when it takes place, it has to be acknowledged as a reality of our brokenness, and compassionately and honestly grieved as such.

I have also suggested that the unquestionable association of romance, coupledom, and happiness is actually damaging to marriages, putting them under more pressure than they sometimes can bear. If they are to weather the storms of changing times and seasons in the relationship, Christian marriages will need a larger framework—that is, their participation in the wider life of the Christian community. If singleness is supported and taken seriously, marriages will be stronger too. When both states are honored and appreciated, fewer people might try to "escape" singleness by hurrying into marriage; and couples may be freed from the pressure of trying to be "everything" for each other, and find freedom and joy in their unique way of participating in the purposes of the kingdom of God. In this larger story, and amongst the new family of God, all are invited to find their own belonging and connection. Whether we are single or married, being and doing family together is an invitation as old as the words of Jesus, and as new as the exciting and daunting world emerging after Christendom.

Finally, despite the title of this book, we would do well to remember that the categories of "singleness" and "marriage" are very broad and helpful only to a point. There are different experiences of being single, depending on whether one is twenty-five or sixty-five, and whether one is an always-single person, or a divorcee, or a widower. The experience of being married also varies depending on the presence or absence of children, one's age, the length of marriage, and so on. Juxtaposing singleness and marriage can be useful for highlighting the problem of valuing one over the other, and for acknowledging the different ways in which human lives can be lived. Yet in light of Jesus' vision, we should strive to make them largely irrelevant as categories: just as there is no longer Jew or Greek, slave or free, male or female, there is also no single or married: "for all of you are one in Christ Jesus" (Gal 3:28).

Bibliography

"10 Keys to Happier Living." https://www.actionforhappiness.org/10-keys-to-happier-living.

Aasgaard, Reidar. *'My Beloved Brothers and Sisters!' Christian Siblingship in Paul.* Early Christianity in Context; Journal for the Study of the New Testament, Supplement Series 265. London: T. & T. Clark, 2004.

Abbott, Elizabeth. *A History of Celibacy.* Cambridge: Lutterworth, 2001.

Abelard, Peter, and Heloise. *The Letters of Abelard and Heloise.* Translated and introduction by Betty Radice. London: Penguin, 2003.

Aercke, Kristiaan P. G. "Anna Bijns: Germanic Sappho." In *Women Writers of the Renaissance and Reformation,* edited by Katharina M. Wilson, 382–83. Athens: University of Georgia Press, 1987.

Alexander, Loveday C. "Sisters in Adversity: Retelling Martha's Story." In *A Feminist Companion to Luke,* edited by Amy-Hill Levine with Marianne Blickenstaff, 197–213. London: Sheffield Academic, 2002.

Allen, Diogenes. *Love: Christian Romance, Marriage, Friendship.* Cambridge: Cowley, 1987.

Allison, Dale C., Jr. *Resurrecting Jesus: The Earliest Christian Tradition and Its Interpreters.* London: Bloomsbury, 2005.

Ambrose. "Concerning Virginity." In *Nicene and Post-Nicene Fathers, Second Series,* translated by H. de Romestin et al., edited by Philip Schaff and Henry Wace, 10:n.p. Buffalo: Christian Literature, 1896. Revised and edited by Kevin Knight. http://www.newadvent.org/fathers/34072.htm.

Andronovienė, Lina. *Transforming the Struggles of Tamars: Single Women and Baptistic Communities.* Eugene, OR: Wipf & Stock, 2014.

"Another Martyr Song by a Woman Who Took her Leave in Rotterdam Together with her Son." Translated by Pamela Klassen. In *Profiles of Anabaptist Women: Sixteenth-Century Reforming Pioneers,* edited by Arnold C. Snyder and Huebert Hecht, 345. Waterloo: Wilfrid Laurier University Press, 2006.

Aquinas, Thomas. *Summa Theologiae.* Translated by Fathers of the English Dominican Province. 1920. http://www.newadvent.org/summa/index.html.

"Article XXV." In *Martyrs Mirror: Of the Defenseless Christians,* 401–2. http://www.homecomers.org/mirror/martyrs055.htm.

Assari, Shervin. "Consensual Sex Is Key to Happiness and Good Health, Science Says." *The Conversation,* February 12, 2018. https://theconversation.com/consensual-sex-is-key-to-happiness-and-good-health-science-says-91384.

Astley, Jeff, and Leslie J. Francis, eds. *Exploring Ordinary Theology: Everyday Christian Believing and the Church*. Aldershot: Ashgate, 2013.

Atkinson, Clarissa W. *The Oldest Vocation: Christian Motherhood in the Middle Ages*. Ithaca: Cornell University Press, 1991.

Augustine, Saint. *Confessions*. Translated by Henry Chadwick. Oxford: Oxford University Press, 1998.

———. "The Good of Marriage." In *Marriage and Sexuality in Early Christianity*. Edited by David G. Hunter, 173–216. Minneapolis: Augsburg Fortress, 2018.

Aune, Kristin. "Singleness and Secularization: British Evangelical Women and Church (Dis)affiliation." In *Women and Religion in the West: Challenging Secularization*, edited by Kristin Aune et al., 57–70. Aldershot: Ashgate, 2008.

———. *Single Women: Challenge to the Church?* Carlisle: Authentic Media, 2002.

Baltensweiler, H. "Eunuch." In *The New International Dictionary of New Testament Theology*, edited by Colin Brown, 1:559–61. Exeter: Paternoster, 1986.

Barber, Matthew, dir. *Give Me Sex Jesus*. Vimeo, 2015. https://vimeo.com/137784146.

Bartchy, Scott S. "Undermining Ancient Patriarchy: The Apostle Paul's Vision of a Society of Siblings." *Biblical Theology Bulletin* 29.2 (1999) 68–78.

Barton, Stephen C. "Finding Happiness in Family Life: Biblical Reflections." *Ex Auditu* 28 (2012) 1–16.

———. *Life Together: Family, Sexuality and Community in the New Testament and Today*. Edinburgh: T. & T. Clark, 2001.

———. "Marriage, Family, the Bible and the Gospel." *Theology* 119.3 (2016) 163–71.

Baumgarten, Joseph M. "Celibacy." In *Encyclopedia of the Dead Sea Scrolls*, edited by Lawrence H. Schiffman and James C VanderKam, 1:122–25. Oxford: Oxford University Press, 2000.

Bearne, Suzanne. "Single Women Are Spending Thousands Freezing Their Eggs—But Is It Worth the Price?" *The Guardian*, March 23, 2019.

Beausobre, Iulia de. *Creative Suffering*. Fairacres, Convent of the Incarnation: SLG, 1984.

Benincasa, Sara. "Psychologists Say Single People Are More Fulfilled. I'm Getting to Understand Why." *The Guardian*, 10 August 2016. https://www.theguardian.com/commentisfree/2016/aug/10/psychology-single-people-more-fulfilled-relationships.

Berger, Peter, et al. *Religious America, Secular Europe? A Theme and Variations*. Aldershot: Ashgate, 2008.

Bernabé, Carmen. "Of Eunuchs and Predators: Matthew 19:1–12 in a Cultural Context." *Biblical Theology Bulletin* 33.4 (November 2003) 128–34.

Betz, Otto. "The Essenes." In *The Cambridge History of Judaism: The Early Roman Period*, edited by William Horbury et al., 3:444–70. Cambridge: Cambridge University Press, 1999.

Bloch, R. Howard. *Medieval Misogyny and the Invention of Western Romantic Love*. Chicago: University of Chicago Press, 1991.

Boesveld, Sarah. "Do Fathers Make Good Mothers? Experts Say Special 'Maternal Instincts' Are a Societal Construct." *National Post*, January 24, 2015. https://nationalpost.com/news/do-fathers-make-good-mothers-the-answer-may-surprise-you.

Bolz-Weber, Nadia. "The Denver Statement." *Sarcastic Lutheran*, August 30, 2017. https://www.patheos.com/blogs/nadiabolzweber/2017/08/the-denver-statement/.

Boswell, John. *Same-Sex Unions in Premodern Europe*. New York: Villard, 1994.

Bowring, Finn. *Erotic Love in Sociology, Philosophy and Literature: From Romanticism to Rationality*. London: Bloomsbury Academic, 2019.

Braght, Van. "The Fifth Letter from Jan Wouterss, to His Wife and Daughter." In *Martyrs Mirror: Of the Defenseless Christians*, 912–15. http://www.homecomers.org/mirror/martyrs132.htm.

Brown, Jonathan. "Isolated: Single Christians Feel Unsupported by Family-focused Churches." *The Independent*, April 24, 2013. http://www.independent.co.uk/news/uk/home-news/isolated-single-christians-feel-unsupported-by-family-focused-churches-8586640.html.

Brown, Peter. *The Body and Society: Men, Women and Sexual Renunciation in Early Christianity*. London: Faber & Faber, 1990.

Bruckner, Pascal. *Perpetual Euphoria: On the Duty to Be Happy*. Translated by Steven Rendall. Princeton: Princeton University Press, 2011.

Byrne, Anne, and Deborah Carr. "Caught in the Cultural Lag: The Stigma of Singlehood." *Psychological Inquiry* 16.2–3 (2005) 84–91.

Cahill, Lisa Sowle. "A Christian Social Perspective on the Family." *The Mennonite Quarterly Review* 75.2 (2001) 161–71.

Cernik, Lizzie. "The Power of Celibacy: 'Giving Up Sex was a Massive Relief.'" *The Guardian*, January 28, 2020. https://www.theguardian.com/lifeandstyle/2020/jan/28/the-power-of-celibacy-giving-up-sex-was-a-massive-relief.

———. "Self-partnered: The Sudden, Surprising Rise of the Single Positivity Movement." *The Guardian*, November 6, 2019. https://www.theguardian.com/lifeandstyle/2019/nov/06/consciously-uncoupled-the-joy-of-self-partnership.

Charles, Tyler. "The Secret Sexual Revolution." *Relevant*, February 20, 2012. http://www.relevantmagazine.com/life/relationship/features/28337-the-secret-sexual-revolution.

Chase, Karen, and Michael Levenson. *The Spectacle of Intimacy: A Public Life for the Victorian Family*. Princeton: Princeton University Press, 2000.

Chilcraft, Steve. *One of Us: Single People as Part of the Church*. Milton Keynes: Word, 1993.

Chilcraft, Steve, et al. *Single Issues: A Whole-church Approach to Singleness*. Warwick: CPAS, 1997.

Chiu, Joyce. "A Single-minded Church." https://www.barna.com/single-minded-church/.

Christian, Diana Leafe. *Creating a Life Together: Practical Tools to Grow Ecovillages and Intentional Communities*. Gabriola Island: New Society, 2003.

Clapp, Rodney. *Families at the Crossroads: Beyond Tradition and Modern Options*. Downers Grove: InterVarsity, 1993.

———. "From Family Values to Family Virtues." In *Virtues and Practices in the Christian Tradition*, edited by Nancey Murphy et al., 186–201. Harrisburg: Trinity, 1997.

Climacus, John. *The Ladder of Divine Ascent*. Translated by Colm Luibheid and Norman Russell. New York: Paulist, 1982.

Coakley, Sarah. *The New Asceticism: Sexuality, Gender and the Quest for God*. London: Bloomsbury, 2015.

Coontz, Stephanie. *Marriage, A History: From Obedience to Intimacy, or How Love Conquered Marriage*. London: Penguin, 2005.

Cooper, Kate. *The Fall of the Roman Household*. Cambridge: Cambridge University Press, 2007.

Coser, Rose, and Lewis A. Coser. "Stay Home, Little Sheba: On Placement, Displacement, and Social Change." *Social Problems* 22 (1975) 470–80.

Craigie, Peter C, et al. *Jeremiah 1–25*. Grand Rapids: HarperCollins, 2016.

Crompton, Louis. *Homosexuality and Civilization*. London: Harvard University Press, 2003.

Csikszentmihalyi, Mihaly. *Flow: The Classic Work on How to Achieve Happiness*. London: Rider, 2002.

Dalfonzo, Gina. *One by One: Welcoming the Singles in Your Church*. Grand Rapids: Baker, 2017.

David, Susan, et al., eds. *Oxford Handbook of Happiness*. Oxford: Oxford University Press, 2012.

Davies, W. D., and Dale C. Allison Jr. *Matthew 19–28*. International Critical Commentary 3. London: Bloomsbury, 1997.

De Groot, Julie, et al., eds. *Single Life and the City 1200–1900*. Basingstoke: Palgrave Macmillan, 2015.

Deming, Will. *Paul on Marriage and Celibacy: The Hellenistic Background of 1 Corinthians 7*. 2nd ed. Grand Rapids: Eerdmans, 2004.

Demir, Meliksah. "Introduction to Relationships and Happiness." In *Oxford Handbook of Happiness*, edited by Susan David et al., 877–80. Oxford: Oxford University Press, 2012.

Demir, Meliksah, et al. "Friendship and Happiness." In *Oxford Handbook of Happiness*, edited by Susan David et al., 921–32. Oxford: Oxford University Press, 2012.

Demos, John P. *A Little Commonwealth: Family Life in Plymouth Colony*. 2nd ed. Oxford: Oxford University Press, 2000.

DePaulo, Bella M. *Marriage vs. Single Life: How Science and the Media Got It So Wrong*. Self-published, CreateSpace, 2015. Kindle.

———. *Singlism: What It Is, Why It Matters, and How to Stop It*. New York: Double Door, 2011.

DePaulo, Bella M., and Wendy L. Morris. "Should Singles and the Scholars Who Study Them Make Their Mark or Stay in Their Place?" *Psychological Inquiry* 16.2–3 (2005) 145–46.

———. "Singles in Society and in Science." *Psychological Inquiry* 16.2–3 (2005) 57–83.

Diognetus. Translated by Alexander Roberts and James Donaldson. In *Ante-Nicene Fathers*, edited by Alexander Roberts et al., 1:n.p. Buffalo: Christian Literature, 1885. Revised and edited by Kevin Knight. http://www.newadvent.org/fathers/0101.htm.

Dixon, Suzanne. *The Roman Family*. Baltimore: Johns Hopkins University Press, 1992.

Dolan, Paul. *Happy Ever After: Escaping the Myth of the Perfect Life*. London: Allen Lane, 2019.

"Do Single Christians Feel Part of Their Churches?" https://www.singlefriendlychurch.com/what-do-single-christians-say-about-church/church-acceptance-1.

Dunn, James D. G. "The Household Rules in the New Testament." In *The Family in Theological Perspective*, edited by Stephen C. Barton, 43–63. Edinburgh: T. & T. Clark, 1996.

Egan, Harvey D. *An Anthology of Christian Mysticism*. 2nd ed. Collegeville: Liturgical, 1996.

Ehrman, Bart D., ed. *Lost Scriptures: Books that Did Not Make It into the New Testament*. Oxford: Oxford University Press, 2003

Elliott, Dyan. "Chastity and Chaste Marriage." In *Women and Gender in Medieval Europe: An Encyclopedia*, edited by Margaret Schaus, 122–24. New York: Routledge, 2006.

———. *Spiritual Marriage: Sexual Abstinence in Medieval Wedlock*. Princeton: Princeton University Press, 1993.

Epictetus. *Discourses. Book III*. Translated by W. A. Oldfather. Cambridge: Harvard University Press, 1928.

Ferguson, Everett. *Backgrounds of Early Christianity*. 2nd ed. Grand Rapids: Eerdmans, 1993.

Fiddes, Paul S. *The Creative Suffering of God*. Oxford: Clarendon, 1988.

Fields, Anna. "*The Atlantic* Got It Wrong: Marriage Is Alive and Well—in the Red States." *Daily Beast*, October 29, 2011. https://www.thedailybeast.com/the-atlantic-got-it-wrong-marriage-is-alive-and-wellin-the-red-states.

Francis, Andrew. *Hospitality and Community After Christendom*. Milton Keynes: Paternoster, 2012.

Francis-Tan, Andrew, and Hugo M. Mialon. "'A Diamond Is Forever' and Other Fairy Tales: The Relationship Between Wedding Expenses and Marriage Duration." *Economic Inquiry* 53.4 (2015) 1919–30.

Frend, W. H. C. "Persecutions: Genesis and Legacy." In *The Cambridge History of Christianity: Origins to Constantine*, edited by Margaret M. Mitchell and Frances M. Young, 1:503–23. Cambridge: Cambridge University Press, 2006.

Gaddini, Katie. "Why Are So Many Single Women Leaving the Church?" *Relevant*, April 28, 2020. https://relevantmagazine.com/god/church/why-are-so-many-single-women-are-leaving-the-church/.

Gibb, Lorna. *Childless Voices: Stories of Longing, Loss, Resistance and Choice*. London: Granta, 2019.

Giddens, Anthony. *The Transformation of Intimacy: Sexuality, Love and Eroticism in Modern Societies*. Stanford: Stanford University Press, 1992.

Gilliam, Connally. *Revelations of a Single Woman: Loving the Life I Didn't Expect*. Carol Stream, IL: SaltRiver, 2006.

Gillis, John R. *A World of Their Own Making: Myth, Ritual, and the Quest for Family Values*. Cambridge: Harvard University Press, 1997.

Goering, Elizabeth M., and Andrea Krause. "Odd Wo/Man Out: The Systematic Marginalization of Mennonite Singles by the Church's Focus on Family." *The Mennonite Quarterly Review* 75.2 (2001) 211–30.

Goertz, Hans-Jürgen. *The Anabaptists*. Translated by Trevor Johnson. London: Routledge, 1996.

Green, Joel B. *The Gospel of Luke*. The New International Commentary of the New Testament. Grand Rapids: Eerdmans, 1997.

Grieser, Jonathan D. "A Tale of Two Convents: Nuns and Anabaptists in Münster, 1533–1535." *Sixteenth Century Journal* 26.1 (1995) 31–47.

Griswold, Charles L., Jr. "Happiness, Tranquillity, and Philosophy." *In Pursuit of Happiness*, edited by Leroy S. Rouner, 13–37. Boston University Studies in Philosophy and Religion 16. Notre Dame: University of Notre Dame Press, 1995.

Grossman, Joanna L., and Lawrence M. Friedman. "Two's Company: How About Three or More?" *Verdict Justia*, June 4, 2020. https://verdict.justia.com/2020/06/04/twos-company-how-about-three-or-more.

Grzymała-Busse, Anna. *Nations under God: How Churches Use Moral Authority to Influence Policy*. Princeton: Princeton University Press, 2015.

Gushee, David P. *Changing Our Minds*. 3rd ed. Canton: Read The Spirit, 2017.

Hajnal, John. "European Marriage Patterns in Perspective." In *Population in History: Essays in Historical Demography*, edited by David Glass and D. E. C. Eversley, 101–43. Chicago: Aldine, 1965.

Hall, Ellie. "Elizabeth Smart: Cultural Obsession With Purity Makes Rape Victims Feel 'Worthless.'" *BuzzFeed News*, May 6, 2013. https://www.buzzfeednews.com/article/ellievhall/elizabeth-smart-obsession-with-purity-makes-rape-victims-fee.

Harding, Linda. *Better Than or Equal To? A Look at Singleness*. Milton Keynes: Word, 1993.

Harris, Josh. "A Statement on *I Kissed Dating Goodbye*." https://joshharris.com/statement/.

Harrison, Carol. "The Silent Majority: The Family in Patristic Thought." In *The Family in Theological Perspective*, edited by Stephen C. Barton, 87–105. Edinburgh: T. & T. Clark, 1996.

Haslett, Adam. "Love Supreme: Gay Nuptials and the Making of Modern Marriage." *The New Yorker*, May 23, 2004. https://www.newyorker.com/magazine/2004/05/31/love-supreme.

Hauerwas, Stanley. *Matthew*. Grand Rapids: Brazos, 2007.

Hauerwas, Stanley, and William H. Willimon. *Where Resident Aliens Live: Exercises for Christian Practice*. Nashville: Abingdon, 1996.

Hawkins, Alan J., and Betsy Vandenberghe. "Divorce Rates Are Falling, but Put a Hold on the Celebration." *National Review*, October 31, 2019. https://www.nationalreview.com/2019/10/divorce-rates-fall-but-young-adults-disadvantaged-couples-still-at-risk/.

Haybron, Dan. "Happiness." In *The Stanford Encyclopedia of Philosophy* (Winter 2019 edition), edited by Edvard N. Zalta. https://plato.stanford.edu/archives/win2019/entries/happiness/.

Hellerman, Joseph H. *When the Church Was a Family: Recapturing Jesus's Vision for Authentic Christian Community*. Nashville: B&H, 2008.

Hill, Wesley. *Washed and Waiting: Reflections on Christian Faithfulness and Homosexuality*. Grand Rapids: Zondervan, 2010.

Hitchcock, Christina S. *The Significance of Singleness: A Theological Vision for the Future of the Church*. Grand Rapids: Baker Academic, 2018.

Horrell, David G. "From ἀδελφοί to οἶκος θεοῦ: Social Transformation in Pauline Christianity." *Journal of Biblical Literature* 120.2 (2001) 293–311.

Howard, Evan B. "The Beguine Option: A Persistent Past and a Promising Future of Christian Monasticism." *Religions* 10.9 (2019) 1–24. https://www.mdpi.com/2077-1444/10/9/491.

Hunt, Margaret R. "The Sapphic Strain: English Lesbians in the Long Eighteenth Century." In *Singlewomen in the European Past, 1250–1800*, edited by Judith Bennett and Amy Froide, 270–96. Philadelphia: University of Pennsylvania Press, 1999.

Hunter, David G. *Marriage and Sexuality in Early Christianity*. Minneapolis: Augsburg Fortress, 2018.

Hutson, Christopher R. "'Saved through Childbearing': The Jewish Context of 1 Timothy 2:15." *Novum Testamentum* 56.4 (2014) 392–410.

Ilarion. "Papyrus Oxyrhynchus." APIS translation. http://papyri.info/ddbdp/p.oxy;4;744.

Ingraham, Christopher. "The Share of Americans Not Having Sex Has Reached a Record High." *The Washington Post*, March 29, 2019. https://www.washingtonpost.com/business/2019/03/29/share-americans-not-having-sex-has-reached-record-high/.

Instone-Brewer, David. *Divorce and Remarriage in the Bible: The Social and Literary Context*. Grand Rapids: Eerdmans, 2002.

Jeeves, Malcolm. "The Nature of Persons and the Emergence of Kenotic Behaviour." In *The Work of Love: Creation as Kenosis*, edited by John Polkinghorne, 66–89. London: SPCK, 2001.

Jelsma, Auke. *Frontiers of the Reformation: Dissidence and Orthodoxy in Sixteenth-century Europe*. Aldershot: Ashgate, 1998.

Jerome. "Against Jovinianus: Book 1." In *Nicene and Post-Nicene Fathers, Second Series*, translated by W. H. Fremantle et al., edited by Philip Schaff and Henry Wace, 6:n.p. Revised and edited by Kevin Knight. http://www.newadvent.org/fathers/30091.htm.

Josephus. *Jewish War*. In *The Genuine Works of Flavius Josephus the Jewish Historian*, translated by William Whiston, n.p. 1737. http://penelope.uchicago.edu/josephus/war-2.html.

———. *The Life of Flavius Josephus*. Translated by William Whiston. http://www.ccel.org/j/josephus/works/autobiog.htm.

Justin Martyr. *The First Apology*. In *Ante-Nicene Fathers*, translated by Marcus Dods and George Reith and edited by Alexander Roberts et al. Revised and edited by Kevin Knight. http://www.newadvent.org/fathers/0126.htm.

Karant-Nunn, Susan C., and Merry E. Wiesner-Hanks. *Luther on Women: A Sourcebook*. Cambridge: Cambridge University Press, 2003.

Keay, Kathy. *Letters from a Solo Survivor*. London: Hodder & Stoughton, 1991.

Keen, Karen R. *Scripture, Ethics, and the Possibility of Same-Sex Relationships*. Grand Rapids: Eerdmans, 2018.

Kislev, Elyakim. "Happiness, Post-Materialist Values, and the Unmarried." *Journal of Happiness Studies* 19.8 (2018) 2243–65.

Kotter-Grühn, Dana, et al. "What Is It We Are Longing For? Psychological and Demographic Factors Influencing the Contents of Sehnsucht (Life Longings)." *Journal of Research in Personality* 43.3 (2009) 428–37.

Kowaleski, Maryanne. "Singlewomen in Medieval and Early Modern Europe: The Demographic Perspective." In *Singlewomen in the European Past, 1250–1800*, edited by Judith Bennett and Amy Froide, 38–81. Philadelphia: University of Pennsylvania Press, 1999.

Kraemer, Ross Shepard, and Mary Rose D'Angelo. *Women and Christian Origins*. New York: Oxford University Press, 1999.

Krawiec, Rebecca. *Shenoute and the Women of the White Monastery: Egyptian Monasticism in Late Antiquity*. Oxford: Oxford University Press, 2002.

Krueger, Derek. "Homoerotic Spectacle and the Monastic Body in Symeon the New Theologian." In *Toward a Theology of Eros: Transfiguring Passion at the Limits of Discipline*, edited by Virginia Burrus and Catherine Keller, 99–118. New York: Fordham University Press, 2006.

LaFosse, Mona Tokarek. "Women, Children and House Churches." In *The Early Christian World*, edited by Philip F. Esler, 385–405. 2nd ed. London: Routledge, 2017.

Layard, Richard. *Happiness: Lessons from a New Science*. Rev. 2nd ed. Penguin, 2011. Kindle ed.

Lee, A. D. *Pagans and Christians in Late Antiquity: A Sourcebook*. London: Routledge, 2000.

"The Legality of Cohabitation Around the World." *Lawyer Monthly*, March 27, 2020. https://www.lawyer-monthly.com/2020/03/the-legality-of-cohabitation-around-the-world/.

Levitan, Kathrin. "Redundancy, the 'Surplus Woman' Problem, and the British Census, 1851–1861." *Women's History Review* 17.3 (2008) 359–76.

Lucas, Richard E., and Andrew E. Clark. "Do People Really Adapt to Marriage?" *Journal of Happiness Studies* 7.4 (2006) 405–26.

Lull, Timothy F., and William R. Russell. *Martin Luther's Basic Theological Writings*. 3rd ed. Minneapolis: Augsburg Fortress, 2012.

Luther, Martin. *Luther: Letters of Spiritual Counsel*. Edited and translated by Theodore G. Tappert. The Library of Christian Classics 18. London: SCM, 1955.

Lutz, Ulrich. *Matthew 8–20*. Hermeneia—A Critical and Historical Commentary on the Bible. Minneapolis: Fortress, 2001.

Lynch, Katherine A. *Individuals, Families, and Communities in Europe, 1200–1800: The Urban Foundations of Western Society*. Cambridge Studies in Population, Economy and Society in Past Time 37. Cambridge: Cambridge University Press, 2003.

MacDonald, Margaret Y. "Reading 1 Corinthians through the Eyes of Families." In *Text, Image, and Christians in the Graeco-Roman World: A Festschrift in Honor of David Lee Balch*, edited by Aliou Cissé Niang and Carolyn Osiek, 38–52. Princeton Theological Monograph Series 176. Eugene, OR: Pickwick, 2012.

Mackin, Theodore. "The Primitive Christian Understanding of Marriage." In *Perspectives on Marriage: A Reader*, edited by Kieran Scott and Michael Warren, 22–28. 3rd ed. Oxford: Oxford University Press, 2007.

Malone, Mary T. *Women and Christianity, Volume III: From the Reformation to the 21st Century*. New York: Orbis, 2003.

"Marcella Pattyn." *The Telegraph*, May 16, 2013. https://www.telegraph.co.uk/news/obituaries/10062339/Marcella-Pattyn.html.

Marotta, Satia A., and Keren Ladin. "Marital Privilege: Bias against Divorced Patients in Medical Decision-Making." *Group Processes & Intergroup Relations* 23.4 (2020) 612–39.

Marsh, Charles, et al., eds. *Lived Theology: New Perspectives on Method, Style, and Pedagogy*. Oxford: Oxford University Press, 2017.

McArthur, Harvey. "Celibacy in Judaism at the Time of Christian Beginnings." *Andrews University Seminary Studies* 25.2 (1987) 163–81.

McCarthy, David Matzko. *Sex and Love in the Home: A Theology of the Household*. London: SCM, 2004.

McClendon, James William. *Ethics*. Vol. 1 of *Systematic Theology*. Rev. ed. Nashville: Abingdon, 2002.

McClendon, James William, and James M. Smith. *Convictions: Defusing Religious Relativism*. Valley Forge: Trinity, 1994.

McDonnell, Ernest W. *The Beguines and Beghards in Medieval Culture: With Special Emphasis on the Belgian Scene*. New Brunswick: Rutgers University Press, 1954.

McFague, Sallie. *Models of God: Theology for an Ecological, Nuclear Age*. London: SCM, 1987.

McGuire, Meredith. *Lived Religion: Faith and Practice in Everyday Life*. Oxford: Oxford University Press, 2008.

McNamara, Jo Ann. *A New Song: Celibate Women in the First Three Christian Centuries*. New York: Haworth, 1983.

Meeks, Wayne A. "Social and Ecclesial Life of the Earliest Christians." In *The Cambridge History of Christianity: Origins to Constantine*, edited by Margaret M. Mitchell and Frances M. Young, 1:145–76. Cambridge: Cambridge University Press, 2006.

Mehl, Roger. *Society and Love: Ethical Problems of Family Life*. Translated by James H. Farley. Philadelphia: Westminster, 1964.

Moltmann, Jürgen. *Sun of Righteousness, Arise! God's Future for Humanity and the Earth*. Translated by Margaret Kohl. Minneapolis: Fortress, 2010.

Moxnes, Halvor. "What Is Family? Problems in Constructing Early Christian Families." In *Constructing Early Christian Families: Family as Social Reality and Metaphor*, edited by Halvor Moxnes, 13–41. London: Routledge, 1997.

Murphy, Nancey, and George F. R. Ellis. *On the Moral Nature of the Universe: Theology, Cosmology, and Ethics*. Minneapolis: Fortress, 1996.

Murray, Stuart. *Post-Christendom: Church and Mission in a Strange New World*. 2nd ed. Eugene, OR: Cascade, 2018.

Myers, Ched, et al. *"Say to This Mountain": Mark's Story of Discipleship*. 2nd ed. Maryknoll: Orbis, 1997.

Nathan, Geoffrey S. *The Family in Late Antiquity: The Rise of Christianity and the Endurance of Tradition*. London: Routledge, 2000.

Nichols, Joel A., ed. *Marriage and Divorce in a Multicultural Context: Multi-Tiered Marriage and the Boundaries of Civil Law and Religion*. New York: Cambridge University Press, 2012.

Noble, Thomas A., et al., eds. *Marriage, Family and Relationships: Biblical, Doctrinal and Contemporary Perspectives*. London: Apollos, 2017.

Ortiz-Ospina, Esteban. "The Rise of Living Alone: How One-person Households Are Becoming Increasingly Common around the World." *Our World in Data*, December 10, 2019. https://ourworldindata.org/living-alone.

Ortiz-Ospina, Esteban, and Max Roser. "Loneliness and Social Connections (2020)." *Our World in Data*, February 2020. https://ourworldindata.org/social-connections-and-loneliness.

Osiek, Carolyn, and David L. Balch. *Families in the New Testament World: Households and House Churches*. Louisville: Westminster John Knox, 1997.

Osiek, Carolyn, et al. *A Woman's Place: House Churches in Earliest Christianity*. Minneapolis: Fortress, 2006.

Oulton, John Ernest Leonard, and Henry Chadwick, trans. *Alexandrian Christianity*. Vol. 2 of *The Library of Christian Classics*. London: SCM, 1954.

Patterson, Sheron C. "Singles and the Church." *Quarterly Review* 12 (Winter 1992) 45–56.

Perel, Esther. *Mating in Captivity: Reconciling the Erotic and the Domestic*. New York: HarperCollins, 2006.

Philo of Alexandria. *On the Contemplative Life*. In *The Contemplative Life, the Giants, and Selections*, by Philo of Alexandria, translated by David Winston, 39–57. London: SPCK, 1981.

"Philosophy." https://www.singlemothersbychoice.org/about/philosophy/.

Plagnol, Anke. "Subjective Well-being Over the Life Course: Conceptualizations and Evaluations." *Social Research* 77.2 (2010) 749–68.

Plato. *Symposium*. Translated by Benjamin Jowett. https://www.gutenberg.org/files/1600/1600-h/1600-h.htm.

Poor, Sara S. "Transmission and Impact: Mechtild of Magdeburg's *Das Fliessende Licht der Gottheit.*" In *A Companion to Mysticism and Devotion in Northern Germany in the Late Middle Ages*, edited by Elizabeth Andersen et al., 73–101. Leiden: Brill, 2013.

Porter, Fran. *Women and Men after Christendom: The Dis-Ordering of Gender Relationships.* Crownhill: Authentic Media, 2015.

Porter, Pamela. *Courtly Love in Medieval Manuscripts.* Toronto: University of Toronto Press, 2003.

"Power of Love at Heart of 'Gay Marriage.'" https://phys.org/news/2012-03-power-heart-gay-marriage.html.

Pullinger, David. "Where Are All the Men? Facts and Stats." https://www.singlefriendlychurch.com/what-do-you-say-when/awhere-are-all-the-mena.

"Queen Bees or Working Bees?" *Saturday Review* 8 (November 1859) 575–76.

Quintos, Christopher. "Loner Living – Solitude Is Bliss." *Euromonitor International* (blog), January 25, 2019. https://blog.euromonitor.com/loner-living-solitude-is-bliss/.

Reddy, William M. *The Making of Romantic Love: Longing and Sexuality in Europe, South Asia, and Japan, 900–1200 CE.* Chicago: University of Chicago Press, 2012.

Reed, David Alan. "Paul on Marriage and Singleness: Reading 1 Corinthians with the Augustan Marriage Laws." PhD diss., University of St. Michael's College, 2013.

"Research Co-funded by Single Christians Confirms that the Church Is Not Attracting Enough Single Men into Its Pews." https://www.singlefriendlychurch.com/research/yougov.

Reynolds, Jill. *The Single Woman: A Discursive Investigation.* London: Routledge, 2008.

Reynolds, Philip Lyndon. *Marriage in the Western Church: The Christianization of Marriage During the Patristic and Early Medieval Periods.* Leiden: Brill, 2001.

Roach, Catherine M. *Happily Ever After: The Romance Story in Popular Culture.* Bloomington: Indiana University Press, 2016.

Rogerson, John. "The Family and Structures of Grace in the Old Testament." In *The Family in Theological Perspective*, edited by Stephen C. Barton, 25–42. Edinburgh: T. & T. Clark, 1996.

Rolheiser, Ronald. *Forgotten Among the Lilies: Learning to Love Beyond Our Fears.* New York: Galilee, 2005.

Roth, John D. "Family, Community and Discipleship in the Anabaptist-Mennonite Tradition." *The Mennonite Quarterly Review* 75.2 (2001) 147–60.

Rougemont, Denis de. *Love in the Western World.* Translated by Montgomery Belgion. Revised and augmented edition. Princeton: Princeton University Press, 1983.

Ruether, Rosemary Radford. *Christianity and the Making of the Modern Family.* London: SCM, 2001.

Salisbury, Joyce E. *Church Fathers, Independent Virgins.* London: Verso, 1991.

Sanders, Jack T. *Ethics in the New Testament.* London: SCM, 1975.

Saphire-Bernstein, Shimon, and Shelley E. Taylor. "Close Relationships and Happiness." In *Oxford Handbook of Happiness*, edited by Susan David et al., 881–93. Oxford: Oxford University Press, 2012.

Sarkisian, Natalia, and Naomi Gerstel. "Does Singlehood Isolate or Integrate? Examining the Link between Marital Status and Ties to Kin, Friends, and Neighbors." *Journal of Social and Personal Relationships* 33.3 (2016) 361–84.

———. "Marriage: The Good, the Bad, and the Greedy." *Contexts* 5.4 (2006) 16–21.

Schüssler Fiorenza, Elisabeth. *In Memory of Her: A Feminist Theological Reconstruction of Christian Origins.* London: SCM, 1983.

Seim, Turid Karlsen. *The Double Message: Patterns of Gender in Luke-Acts.* Edinburgh: T. & T. Clark, 1994.

Seligman, Martin E. P. *Authentic Happiness: Using the New Positive Psychology to Realize Your Potential for Lasting Fulfillment.* New York: Free, 2002.

Shaw, Theresa M. "Sex and Sexual Renunciation I." In *The Early Christian World,* edited by Philip F. Esler, 355–71. 2nd ed. London: Routledge, 2017.

Sheridan, Jean. *The Unwilling Celibates: A Spirituality for Single Adults.* Mystic: Twenty-Third, 2000.

Simons, Menno. *The Complete Works of Menno Simon.* Elkhart: Funk & Bros, 1871.

Simons, Walter. "On the Margins of Religious Life: Hermits and Recluses, Penitents and Tertiaries, Beguines and Beghards." In *The Cambridge History of Christianity,* edited by Miri Rubin and Walter Simons, 309–23. Cambridge: Cambridge University Press, 2009.

"Single-minded: Single People in the Church." *Administry Resource Paper* 92.4 (1992).

Smith, James K. A. *You Are What You Love: The Spiritual Power of Habit.* Grand Rapids: Brazos, 2016.

Soranus of Ephesus. *Soranus' Gynecology.* Translated by Owsei Temkin. Baltimore: Johns Hopkins University Press, 1991.

Sorrell, Karissa Knox. "The Dangers of Purity Culture." *Mutuality,* September 9, 2015. https://www.cbeinternational.org/resource/article/mutuality-blog-magazine/dangers-purity-culture.

Sprinkle, Preston, ed. *Two Views on Homosexuality, the Bible, and the Church.* Grand Rapids: Zondervan, 2016.

Sprinkle, Preston, and Branson Parler. "Polyamory: Pastors' Next Sexual Frontier." *Christianity Today,* September 25, 2019. https://www.christianitytoday.com/pastors/2019/fall/polyamory-next-sexual-frontier.html.

Stark, Rodney. *The Rise of Christianity: How the Obscure, Marginal Jesus Movement Became the Dominant Religious Force in the Western World in a Few Centuries.* San Francisco: HarperCollins, 1997.

Stone, Lyman. "Sex Ratios in the Pews: Is There Really a Deficit of Men in American Churches?" *Institute for Family Studies,* August 12, 2019. https://ifstudies.org/blog/sex-ratios-in-the-pews-is-there-really-a-deficit-of-men-in-american-churches.

Stoner, Abby. "Sisters Between: Gender and Medieval Beguines." https://history.sfsu.edu/sites/default/files/EPF/1995_Abby%20Stoner-ilovepdf-compressed.pdf.

Strawn, Brent A. "The Triumph of Life: Towards a Biblical Theology of Happiness." In *The Bible and the Pursuit of Happiness,* edited by Brent A. Strawn, 287–322. Oxford: Oxford University Press, 2012.

Stutzer, Alois, and Bruno S. Frey. "Does Marriage Make People Happy, or Do Happy People Get Married?" *Journal of Socio-Economics* 35.2 (2006) 326–47.

Tacitus. *The Annals.* Translated by John Jackson. Loeb Classical Library 4. Cambridge: Harvard University Press, 1937.

Talbot, Alice-Mary. "The Byzantine Family and the Monastery." *Dumbarton Oaks Papers* 44 (1990) 119–29.

Tertullian. *To His Wife.* Translated by S. Thelwall. Edited by Alexander Roberts et al. Revised and edited by Kevin Knight. http://www.newadvent.org/fathers/0404.htm.

Thane, Pat. *Happy Families? History and Family Policy.* London: British Academy, 2011.

Thiselton, Anthony C. *The First Epistle to the Corinthians.* New International Greek Testament Commentary. Grand Rapids: Eerdmans, 2000.

Toth, Lina. "Befriending: Friendship as a Personal, Communal, and Missional Practice." In *Seeds of the Church: Towards an Ecumenical Baptist Ecclesiology*, edited by Henk Bakker et al. Eugene, OR: Wipf & Stock, forthcoming.

Tournier, Paul. *Creative Suffering*. London: SCM, 1985.

Towner, Philip H. *The Letters to Timothy and Titus*. New International Commentary on the New Testament. Grand Rapids: Eerdmans, 2006.

Trebilco, Paul. "Brothers and Sisters – Ἀδελφοί." In *Self-Designations and Group Identity in the New Testament*, 16–67. Cambridge: Cambridge University Press, 2011.

Trimberger, E. Kay. *The New Single Woman*. Boston: Beacon, 2005.

United Nations Department of Economic and Social Affairs, Population Division. "World Marriage Data 2019." https://population.un.org/MarriageData/Index.html#/home.

Voobus, Arthur. *Celibacy, A Requirement for Admission to Baptism in the Early Syrian Church*. Stockholm: Papers of the Estonian Theological Society in Exile, 1951.

Wadell, Paul J. *Becoming Friends: Worship, Justice and the Practice of Christian Friendship*. Grand Rapids: Brazos, 2002.

Wadsworth, Tim. "Marriage and Subjective Well-being: How and Why Context Matters." *Social Indicators Research* 126.3 (2016) 1025–48.

Waite, Linda, and Maggie Gallagher. *The Case for Marriage: Why Married People are Happier, Healthier, and Better Off Financially*. New York: Doubleday, 2000.

Ward, Benedicta. *Bede's Ecclesiastical History of the English People: An Introduction and Selection*. London: Bloomsbury, 2012.

Ward, Hannah, and Jennifer Wild. *Human Rites: Worship Resources for an Age of Change*. London: Mowbray, 1995.

Ward, Pete. *Introducing Practice*. Grand Rapids: Baker Academic, 2017.

Wiesner-Hanks, Merry E. *Christianity and Sexuality in the Early Modern World: Regulating Desire, Reforming Practice*. London: Routledge, 2000.

Wendel, Francois. *Calvin: The Origins and Development of his Religious Though*. Translated by Philip Mairet. London: Collins, 1963.

"What Do Christians Think about Sex before Marriage?" https://www.singlefriendlychurch.com/attitudes-to-single-living/sex-before-marriage.

Williams, Zoe. "'Raw Hatred': Why the 'Incel' Movement Targets and Terrorises Women." *The Guardian*, April 25, 2018. https://www.theguardian.com/world/2018/apr/25/raw-hatred-why-incel-movement-targets-terrorises-women.

Winnail, Douglas S. "Marriage and Family: Vital Institutions in Crisis." *Tomorrow's World*, March–April 2003. https://www.tomorrowsworld.org/magazines/2003/march-april/marriage-and-family-vital-institutions-in-crisis.

Winter, Bruce W. *Roman Wives, Roman Widows: The Appearance of New Women and the Pauline Communities*. Grand Rapids: Eerdmans, 2003.

Witherington, Ben, III. *Matthew*. Smyth & Helwys Bible Commentary. Macon: Smyth & Helwys, 2006.

———. "On the Road with Mary Magdalene, Joanna, Susanna, and Other Disciples—Luke 8.1–3." In *A Feminist Companion to Luke*, edited by Amy-Hill Levine with Marianne Blickenstaff, 133–39. London: Sheffield Academic, 2002.

Printed in Great Britain
by Amazon

79776930R00089